Learning Advanced Python by Studying Open Source Projects

This book is one of its own kind. It is not an encyclopedia or a hands-on tutorial that traps readers in the tutorial hell. It is a distillation of just one common Python user's learning experience. The experience is packaged with exceptional teaching techniques, careful dependence unraveling and, most importantly, passion.

Learning Advanced Python by Studying Open Source Projects helps readers overcome the difficulty in their day-to-day tasks and seek insights from solutions in famous open source projects. Different from a technical manual, this book mixes the technical knowledge, real-world applications and more theoretical content, providing readers with a practical and engaging approach to learning Python.

Throughout this book, readers will learn how to write Python code that is efficient, readable and maintainable, covering key topics such as data structures, algorithms, object-oriented programming and more. The author's passion for Python shines through in this book, making it an enjoyable and inspiring read for both beginners and experienced programmers.

Rongpeng Li (Ron) is a YouTube educator and animator. He has a consistent passion for education. He has published two books on statistics and scientific simulation.

Chapman & Hall/CRC
The Python Series

About the Series

Python has been ranked as the most popular programming language, and it is widely used in education and industry. This book series will offer a wide range of books on Python for students and professionals. Titles in the series will help users learn the language at an introductory and advanced level, and explore its many applications in data science, AI, and machine learning. Series titles can also be supplemented with Jupyter notebooks.

Image Processing and Acquisition using Python, Second Edition
Ravishankar Chityala, Sridevi Pudipeddi

Python Packages
Tomas Beuzen and Tiffany-Anne Timbers

Statistics and Data Visualisation with Python
Jesús Rogel-Salazar

Introduction to Python for Humanists
William J.B. Mattingly

Python for Scientific Computation and Artificial Intelligence
Stephen Lynch

Learning Professional Python
Usharani Bhimavarapu and Jude D. Hemanth

Learning Advanced Python by Studying Open Source Projects
Rongpeng Li

For more information about this series please visit: https://www.crcpress.com/Chapman--HallCRC/book-series/PYTH

Learning Advanced Python by Studying Open Source Projects

Rongpeng Li

CRC Press
Taylor & Francis Group
Boca Raton London New York

CRC Press is an imprint of the
Taylor & Francis Group, an **informa** business

A CHAPMAN & HALL BOOK

Cover image: Rongpeng Li

First edition published 2024
by CRC Press
2385 Executive Center Drive, Suite 320, Boca Raton, FL 33431

and by CRC Press
4 Park Square, Milton Park, Abingdon, Oxon, OX14 4RN

CRC Press is an imprint of Taylor & Francis Group, LLC

© 2024 Rongpeng Li

Library of Congress Cataloging-in-Publication Data
Names: Li, Rongpeng, author.
Title: Learning advanced Python from open source projects / Rongpeng Li.
Description: Boca Raton, FL : CRC Press, 2024. | Series: Chapman & Hall/CRC
the Python series | Includes bibliographical references and index.
Identifiers: LCCN 2023024040 (print) | LCCN 2023024041 (ebook) |
ISBN 9781032328164 (paperback) | ISBN 9781032328188 (hardback) |
ISBN 9781003316909 (ebook)
Subjects: LCSH: Python (Computer program language) | Open source software.
Classification: LCC QA76.73.P98 L49 2024 (print) | LCC QA76.73.P98
(ebook) | DDC 005.13/3—dc23/eng/20230725
LC record available at https://lccn.loc.gov/2023024040
LC ebook record available at https://lccn.loc.gov/2023024041

ISBN: 978-1-032-32818-8 (hbk)
ISBN: 978-1-032-32816-4 (pbk)
ISBN: 978-1-003-31690-9 (ebk)

DOI: 10.1201/9781003316909

Typeset in Minion
by codeMantra

To Yan, the brightest light in my life.
To my family, whose decisions made my life today possible.
To Holly and Prosper, the endless source of joy in the room.

Contents

Preface

I am very excited and happy to present this book to you.

This book is somewhat like my previous two books. Not because they share similar topics, but because I wrote it with a vivid image of readers in my mind. In my opinion, a book like this should have existed long before: there are tons of great open source Python projects, and there are a lot of people who find it hard to learn advanced Python topics. It is natural to have a book that seamlessly bridges the golden resources and the hungry learners. This book is it. When I tried to learn from the pros, I did it the hard way by bashing my head and absorbing much-alike materials from 20 browser tabs. Looking back, I think there are better ways to do it: an educational and instructional way. My experience as an instructor helped me a lot in writing this book: I am able to put my feet in the learners' shoes.

I am very grateful to the editors at Taylor & Francis who helped me identify and confirmed the value of this approach. I hope you find this experimental approach educational, accessible and entertaining.

Acknowledgments

I would like to thank the creators, maintainers and all contributors to the open source projects I used as examples in this book.

It is unimaginable if those amazing resources are not freely accessible to me and to everyone around the globe. The open source movement has astronomically impacted not only the software engineering but also the advance of technology universally.

Thank you, from the bottom of my heart.

Introduction

PURPOSE AND SCOPE OF THIS BOOK

Learning Advanced Python by Studying Open Source Projects is a book that is written for 95% of Python users, covering 95% of their daily use cases.

What does this mean?

From the content perspective, it means that this book is not an encyclopedia that covers everything. It covers all the *important* things for *most* Python users.

Based on my observations and research, the following topics are considered important:

1. The Python data model

2. The Python classes

3. Concurrency and asynchronous programming

4. Functions and related tips

5. How to design an OOP system

6. How to test code

They are important in different ways.

1. The Python data model and Python classes are fundamentally important as they are the basics to learn everything else. They are basic but they are not obviously easy to master. Many Python users, or most Python users didn't graduate with a computer science master's degree. They started using Python by copying and pasting so long as the code worked. At some point in their learning or career path, the lack of foundation will bite. I want to solidify your foundations.

2. The other four topics are deemed as a gap between so-so engineers and more professional engineers. I picked these four because they are the ones that I find easy to break the cyclic dependencies of the advanced topics. For example, it is impossible to talk about concepts like fixture without talking about decorators first. It is hard

DOI: 10.1201/9781003316909-1

to imagine context manager without talking about the idea of coroutine first: well technically you can. I try to chop the open source projects that utilize multiple such concepts into digestible pieces. The example of aiosqlite is probably the most typical example. Please do read Chapter 5 and let me know whether I did an acceptable job.

The following topics are not considered important enough for most readers.

1. Improve Python performance by writing C or C++

2. Publishing a Python package

Well, those topics are very important if you are working on fine-tuning Python performances: not because of bad code but because of Python itself. For example, some high-performance computing work requires such skills, but most Python users don't ever write a line of C in their whole career. Similarly, most people don't publish Python packages as well.

There are great resources on these two topics. I would recommend the official doc for the former and the book *Publishing Python Packages*[1] by Dane Hillard for the latter. Honestly speaking, the fact that the second topic is enough for an independent book also makes it impractical to be included in this book. The first topic is also big enough for an independent book.

The following topics are indeed important, but they are not really Python specific.

1. Documentation

2. Project management and communication

The first draft of this book included documentation as an independent chapter. Popular Python open source libraries often have fabulous documentation. However, the more I wrote about it, the more I feel that they are not *advanced Python*, they are skills related to *advanced Programming*. Everyone who wrote code needs to know them. It is not suitable to include them in a book about Python.

Similar ideas apply to project management. Since most open source projects are developed for the public, you can read the comments, the interactions and sometimes spicy exchanges between developers and users. I personally find this topic super interesting while preparing the materials. However, they are, again, not Python specific. I have to drop it.

Let's discuss the purpose of this book. This book's purpose is to help moderately good Python users to become professional Python users.

What is a Python user? What is moderately good? What makes a Python user professional?

A Python user is a superset of a Python developer. When I was a PhD student, I used Python a lot. I was not a Python developer. Namely, I wrote Python as a tool to do something else, rather than for the sake of writing Python. On the contrary, a Python developer's job is to write high-quality Python applications.

However, I find Python users' work often requires very high technical skills. For example, a Jupyter Notebook is far from enough for a researcher. The researchers sometimes *hack* their way through the development and write terrible code. This book aims at the aspirational and ambitious Python users so they can use Python in the most efficient way. Of course, developers are welcome.

So, what is exactly being *moderately* good that qualifies you to read this book?

If you

1. have day-to-day experience writing Python code to perform tasks like string manipulation and tabulated data processing.

2. are familiar with basic object-oriented programming concepts like class, instance and inheritance.

3. understand basic operating system concepts like process, thread and memory.

4. are familiar with tools/platforms like Git, GitHub and VS Code.

Then, you are considered moderately good. Sounds easy, right?

What makes a Python user professional? This is important as it is what you will gradually learn to become while reading this book.

A professional user can, not limited to the list though, perform the following tasks:

1. read code written by others *efficiently* and *correctly*.

2. write more robust, elegant and well-tested Python code.

3. have a deep understanding of Python's data model and use it *appropriately*.

4. know how to design an OOP system and turn it into reality.

I hope this gives a good idea of what topics this book covers, and what kind of prerequisites I am expecting the readers to have.

OVERVIEW OF THE APPROACH TAKEN

One of the biggest features of this book is that it is not written in a textbook style. Instead, it is written somewhat like a novel as long as the circumstance permits.

In a textbook, the author introduces the concepts, then the theorems, then the solved examples, followed by exercises.

In a novel, a character doesn't get on the stage until it is time for the character. The plot has its own rhythm, and characters have natural development paths.

In this book, concepts and best practices are not introduced until it becomes evident and obvious that they are absolutely needed. For example, the idea of mixin is not introduced until we find the class relationship in scikit-learn becomes error-prone and unmanageable. This is how humans learn. Newton's laws are not written as a bullet list. They are discovered after countless observations, experiments and calculations.

Here is another more detailed example.

You want to write a test that tests whether the tested function writes some output to the screen. You are not sure how to do it so you Google it.

Google returns some links and you click in. Several pages mention the idea of monkey patch but the code examples in the StackOverflow links are so complex that you can't use them directly. You try to read the official docs and it is so long. You try to search on GitHub but there are decorators on top of decorators with weird syntax. You give up.

What this book offers is a guidance to smoothen the path from the problem to the answer. I will explain why monkey patch is introduced in testing, what problems it tries to resolve and how it solves it. I have carefully designed the order of the topics in this book so you will already have a good grasp of the Python data model before using the, say, *setattr()* function doing monkey patching. Then I will show you that the problems you are facing also exist in the big-name open source projects. We will study how they solve the problems and the solution to your own problem will be self-revealing.

I do acknowledge that sometimes the order has to be reversed if the example in the open source project is too complex to absorb at the beginning. I will provide a solution to your problems first then move on to the open source counterparts.

Again, I am very excited that you picked up this highly experimental book. I hope you enjoy it and I look forward to your feedback.

NOTE

1 Dane Hillard. Publishing Python Package. Dec 2022. NY: Manning.

## CHAPTER 1

The Data Model of Python ◆

A GENTLE INTRODUCTION TO PYTHON'S DATA MODEL

Have you wondered what makes a Python *dict* a dictionary, and what makes a Python *list* a list? In Python, you can perform different kinds of operations on different kinds of data structures. Take a *list*, for example, you can append a member to a list, *extend* one list with another one and *index* it with integers. Let's build a list of cars with code snippet 1.1.

```
cars = list()
cars.append('bmw')
cars.extend(['audi', 'toyota'])
assert cars[0] == 'bmw'
last_car = cars.pop()
assert last_car == 'toyota'
assert len(cars) == 2
```

CODE 1.1   Operations on a Python list object.[1]

For a dictionary, you can perform a different set of operations as shown in code snippet 1.2. You can *get* a member of the dictionary. Note that both *list* and *dict* support the *len()* method.

```
fruit_prices = dict()
fruit_prices['apple'] = 0.5
fruit_prices['orange'] = 0.25
assert len(fruit_prices) == 2
assert fruit_prices.get('pear') == None
```

CODE 1.2   Operations with a Python *dict* object.

What makes lists and dictionaries behave in different ways? What if we want to modify their behaviors and create a hybrid data structure to suit our needs? This will be the main topic of this chapter: the data model[2] for built-in Python data types.

DOI: 10.1201/9781003316909-2

In Python, everything is an instance of the object class. You can think of object as the ancestor of all *things* in Python, including the built-in types like *int*, *str*, *list*, *dict* and all user-defined classes. Let's try some examples with code snippet 1.3.

```
isinstance("California",object)
# True

isinstance(int,object)
# True

isinstance(list(),object)
# True

class Car:
    pass

isinstance(Car(),object)
# True

isinstance(Car, object)
# True
```

CODE 1.3   Check the objects' types with *isinstance()* function.

A *Car* instance is an object instance. Also, the *Car* class itself is an object instance. The question is that if all *stuffs* are instances of the object class, then what makes a *list* different from a *dict*?

Let's check the supported methods of a *list* and a *dict*.

The *dir()* function returns a list of attributes and methods supported by an object. We sort the list in alphabetical order to make it easier to compare the results. Code snippet 1.4 shows the result for a list instance.

```
sorted(dir(list()))

# ['__add__',  '__class__',  '__class_getitem__',  '__contains__',
'__delattr__',  '__delitem__',  '__dir__',  '__dir__',  '__doc__',
'__eq__',  '__format__',  '__ge__',  ...] # skipped
```

CODE 1.4   The attributes and methods supported by a Python list object.

Let's check what methods are supported by a *list* instance but not supported by a *dict* instance and vice versa. To do that, we need to build two sets and take a difference as shown in code snippet 1.5.

```
set(dir(list())) - set(dir(dict()))
```

```
# {`__add__', `__iadd__', `__imul__', `__mul__', `__rmul__',
`append', `count', `extend', `index', `insert', `remove',
`reverse', `sort'}

# the other way around

set(dir(dict())) - set(dir(list()))
# {`__ior__', `__or__', `__ror__', `fromkeys', `get',
`items', `keys', `popitem', `setdefault', `update', `values'}
```

CODE 1.5   Compare the differences of supported methods for a list and a set.

You may notice that both *list* and *set* support the __gt__ methods. It means that you can compare two lists or two dictionaries. It seems that they follow the same *protocol* here that defines what they can do: they can be compared against their own kinds.

However, a list supports the __add__ method while a *dict* instance does not. This hints that they follow different protocols: lists can be added directly, while dictionaries cannot.

In the following sections, you will learn how to create your own data structures that follow different protocols and control exactly how they behave.

CUSTOMIZED COMPARISON

Let's begin with a scenario. You are hired by a major car dealer to create an application that will help them to keep track of their customers' information. One key feature of the application is to compare the in-house creditability of customers. For example, if two customers bid for the same car, the application needs to tell your boss which customer is more credible.

We need a *Customer* class. Code snippet 1.6 creates it.

```
class Customer:
    def __init__(self, first_name: str, last_name: str, credit_
score: int, credit_limit: int, in_debt: bool, monthly_income: int):
        self.first_name = first_name
        self.last_name = last_name
        self.credit_score = credit_score
        self.credit_limit = credit_limit
        self.in_debt = in_debt
        self.monthly_income = monthly_income

    def __repr__(self):
        debt_status = "not in debt" if self.in_debt == False else
"in debt"
        return f"Customer {self.first_name} {self.last_name},
{debt_status}," \
            f" with a credit score of {self.credit_score},"\
            f" credit limit of {self.credit_limit}" \
            f" and a monthly income of {self.monthly_income}."
```

```
        f"with a credit score of {self.credit_score},"\
            f"credit limit of {self.credit_limit}" \
            f"and a monthly income of {self.monthly_income}."
```

CODE 1.6   The *Customer* class.

The __*repr*__ method is used to print the object. If you don't define it, Python will print the object's memory address like < __main__.Customer object at0x1083c4ee0>. We can create a few customers and play around with them as shown in code snippet 1.7.

```
john_smith = Customer("John", "Smith", 800, 200000, False, 10000)
richard_dawkins = Customer("Richard", "Dawkins", 700, 240000,
True, 8000)
albert_jackson = Customer("Albert", "Jackson", 700, 250000, True,
12000)
melissa_miller = Customer("Melissa", "Miller", 700, 250000, False,
9000)

print(melissa_miller)
# Customer Melissa Miller, not in debt, with a credit score of
700, credit limit of 250000 and a monthly income of 9000.
```

CODE 1.7   Create a few customers and print one out.

To compare the financial credibility of the customers, the car dealer has created a set of rules based on their historical experiences. The rules are organized in order such that the rules are checked in order. These rules are:

1. The customer with a higher credit score is more credible.

2. When credit scores are equal, the customer with a higher credit limit is more credible.

3. When both are equal, the customer with a higher monthly income is more credible.

However, if the one who gets paid higher is in debt while another who gets paid lower is not, the difference of monthly income must be larger than 4000. Otherwise, the one who is not in debt is more credible.

Ideally, we want to compare the *john _ smith* and *richard _ dawkins* objects in code snippet 1.8. However, we can't do it because *Customers* don't support such operations.

```
john_smith < richard_dawkins
# Traceback (most recent call last):
#   File "FILE_PATH", line 25, in <module>
#   john_smith < richard_dawkins
# TypeError: '<' not supported between instances of 'Customer' and
'Customer'
```

CODE 1.8   Comparison is not supported for the *Customer* class.

We have two solutions. One is to write a helper function that compares two customers. Every time we need to compare customers, we can pass the function to something like the *key* parameter of the *sort()* method. Another solution is to enable native support for *Customer* comparison.

> Which solution is better? The logic of comparison needs to go somewhere in the code. The question is where. The canonical way is in the *Customer* class. There are two reasons. First, by enabling syntax like *john _ smith < richard _ dawkins*, we aligned our syntax with the Pythonic way of doing comparison. It is much easier for your coworkers to integrate the code into their projects. Second, the built-in comparison logic is more robust and error-free than a standalone function. When you ship your code to someone else, you have a better control over the code unless the code users deliberately overwrite the comparison logic in the *Customer* class, which is much less likely than them writing another standalone comparison function.

Let's pause our concerns for a while to learn from the pros and see how this is done in the *SymPy* library. *SymPy* is an open source Python library for symbolic computation. It can be used to perform algebraic computations and symbolic differentiation, etc. Code snippet 1.9 shows a differentiation example.

```
import sympy as sym
x = sym.symbols("x")
print(type(x))
# <class 'sympy.core.symbol.Symbol'>
print(sym.diff(x**2+sym.sin(x) + 2*x,x))
# 2*x + cos(x) + 2
```

CODE 1.9   Use *SymPy* to calculate the derivative of a function.

In snippet 1.9, we defined a symbol x and differentiated the expression $x^2 + sin(x) + 2x$, the result is correct: $2x + cos(x) + 2$.

Like our cases, customized comparisons are also common in *SymPy*. For example, a polynomial's terms can be arranged in any order, but the polynomial remains the same. We would love to enable such mathematical expression comparison.

In Python, *magic* methods or *dunder* methods like __*lt*__ and __*ge*__ define how comparisons are done. The first stands for *less than*, and the latter stands for *greater than or equal to*. Redefining them, in other programming languages, is often called *operating overloading*.

> Dunder is an abbreviation of *double underscore* if you are wondering.

Back to *SymPy*, instead of studying its implementation, let's investigate a bug to pierce into its core. The developers found a bug that alternating two objects' order in comparison gives different results in early 2021. As stated in issue 20796,[3] the two comparisons in code snippet 1.10 should both return *False*. Based on the types of them, one represents numerical value and another logical. Objects with different data types should always be different.

```
from sympy import S

S(0.0) == S.false
# True

S.false == S(0.0)
# False
```

CODE 1.10   Singleton comparisons in *SymPy*.

S here stands for *Singleton*. `S.false` means that there is only one such thing as a *mathematical false* in the whole mathematical universe. There can only be one *false* and there can only be one *0*.

> In object-oriented programming, a singleton is a design pattern that restricts the instantiation of a class to a single instance and ensures that there is a global point of access to that instance.
> `S.EmptySet` is a singleton example that represents THE mathematical empty set. It is handy to use a singleton object to represent a special value in mathematics because this empty set is just that empty set, there are no two different empty sets nor two different infinities.

Now, let's get to the implementation of the ___eq___ method of the *S* class. Pull request 20801[4] fixed the issue but I already copied the pre-PR implementation to snippet 1.11.

In snippet 1.11, the `self` represents a float number.

```
def __eq__(self, other):
    from sympy.logic.boolalg import Boolean
    try:
        other = _sympify(other)
    except SympifyError:
        return NotImplemented
    if not self:  # comment 1
        return not other
    if isinstance(other, Boolean):  # comment 2
        return False
    if other.is_NumberSymbol:
        if other.is_irrational:
            return False
        return other.__eq__(self)
    if other.is_Float:
        # comparison is exact
        # so Float(.1, 3) != Float(.1, 33)
```

```
        return self._mpf_ == other._mpf_
    if other.is_Rational:
        return other.__eq__(self)
    if other.is_Number:
        ompf = other._as_mpf_val(self._prec)
        return bool(mlib.mpf_eq(self._mpf_, ompf))
    return False   # Float != non-Number
```

CODE 1.11 Equality comparison of a float number with a bool, before pull request 20801.

The __eq__ method takes two arguments, the first one is the object itself and the second one is the object to be compared with. When you write comparison like *A* == B, The __eq__ method of the object on the left side of the comparison is called: in the example, *A*.

In the line denoted with comment 1, we first check the Boolean representation of the object itself. If it is *False*, it means the object is a 0, probably with arbitrary precision. In that case, we check the other object. If it is also equivalent to 0, then they are equal.

In the line denoted with comment 2, we check whether the other object is a *Boolean* object or not. If it is, then we always return *False*. A number is never the same with a *Boolean*, mathematically.

A quick note if you are not catching up. How did we know that the float number's __eq__ method is wrong? Since *S.false* == *S(0.0)* gives the correct answer, which is *False*, we then know the *S.false.* __eq__ *(S(0.0))* returns the right answer. This is how we know that the issue is in the implementation of __eq__ for the float number Singleton object.

The devil lies in the order of the two lines I commented. When a float number is equivalent to 0, *not self* in the first if statement is evaluated to be *True*, therefore if the other object is a *False* object, a *True* value is returned. These two if statements need to be switched. If the types are different, then they are never equivalent. This is exactly what the pull request 20801 fixes.

Notice that the practice is very similar to our proposed implementation of __lt__ or __gt__ methods for the Customer class. The order of criteria matters.

Go back on our original question, code snippet 1.12 is implements the __lt__ method for the *Customer* class. It is probably the most elegantly written code. In production, make sure you write comprehensive tests, too.

```
def __lt__(self, other):
    income_threshold = 4000
    if self.credit_score != other.credit_score:
        return self.credit_score < other.credit_score

    if self.credit_limit != other.credit_limit:
        return self.credit_limit < other.credit_limit
    income_diff = abs(self.income - other.income)

    if self.monthly_income < other.monthly_income:
```

```
        if not self.in_debt and other.in_debt:
            return income_diff > income_threshold
        return True
    elif self.monthly_income > other.monthly_income:
        if self.in_debt and not other.in_debt:
            return income_diff < income_threshold
        return False
    else:
        return False
```

CODE 1.12   Implementation of the *less than* logic for `Customer` class.

This dunder method allows users to sort customers natively as shown in code snippet 1.13.

```
john_smith > richard_dawkins
# True

sorted([john_smith, richard_dawkins, albert_jackson, melissa_
miller])[0] == albert_jackson
# True
```

CODE 1.13   Customer instances can be compared directly now.

So far everything looks great. Let's do something even fancier in the next section.

A MANAGED ITERATION BEHAVIOR

Summarizing our first lesson, we get a taste that Python objects, whether built-in or user-defined, can implement or fulfill different *protocols*.

I am being a little lazy with words here to deviate the definition of protocol from a rigorous computer science sense. It basically means a set of rules that defines the behaviors of an object. For example, if you define a `Customer` class with a method `change_credit_limit()`, then we have a rule that says that a `Customer` object can change its credit limit without caring much how it is implemented.

Python's built-in data structures implement different protocols. The `collections.abc`[5] module provides abstract base classes for containers that obey a set of protocols. Here are a few examples from this module.

1. *Sequence*: a sequence is a sequence of members.

2. *MutableSequence*: a sequence whose members can change.

3. *Mapping*: immutable map from keys to values.

4. *MutableMapping*: a Mapping that the mapping relationship can be changed.

Please be aware of the difference between the abstract base class and the abstract base class for containers. The former is a superset of the latter. The abstract base classes in Python also include those from the numbers module and the io module, etc.

Each abstract class is required to have a specific set of abstract methods. A *realization* of one of those abstract classes must implement the corresponding abstract methods.

The abstract classes also have inheritance relationships. For example, the `Reversible` abstract class is a subclass of the `Iterable` abstract class. Therefore, besides the `iter()` method, the `Reversible` class also defines the `reversed()` method. The `Sequence` abstract class is a subclass of both the `Reversible` and the `Collection` abstract classes. Therefore, the Sequence class also needs to define the `len()` method and the `contains()` method to support the `in` operator, as you often see in the `for loop` statements.

By the courtesy of Sangmoon Oh, the inheritance relationship between abstract base classes for containers can be visualized as a hierarchy as shown in Figure 1.1. You can find his blog on Medium.[6]

The reason we are interested in the hierarchy of abstract classes is that sometimes we need to create our own hybrid or Frankenstein classes. Here is the continuation of the car dealership example.

Your employer, the car dealer, is pleased with your work. Now, the managements want you to create an application to store and retrieve customer data according to their VIP status. After some analysis, you identify that you need a data structure to support the

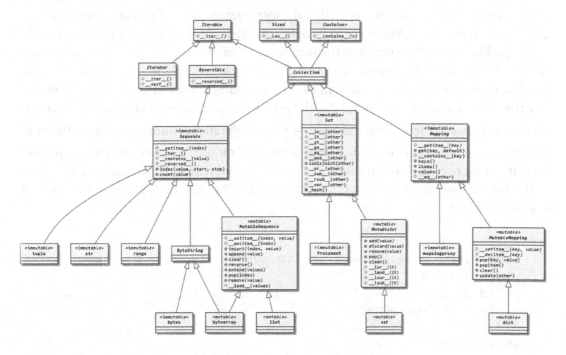

FIGURE 1.1 The class hierarchy of abstract base classes for containers.

following requirements. Let's call such a data structure *CustomerStruct*, which is essentially a container of *Customers*.

1. A *CustomerStruct* should support membership tests in $O(1)$ time.

2. A *CustomerStruct* should support insertion, deletion and union efficiently.

3. A *CustomerStruct* should support iteration in a special way that it always returns the VIP customers first.

If a new car is available, the car dealer can iterate through VIP customers first to give them privileges to choose first. The *CustomerStruct* should largely behave like a set. Among all the common data structures, only dictionaries and sets support membership tests in $O(1)$ time. Since we are not looking up for data, a set is enough. The issue with a default set is that its iteration is not in any particular order after some member manipulation. However, you should know that since Python 3.7, the default *dict* data structure is insertion-ordered if you iterate over a dictionary. I will quote from the Python documentation:

> A set is an unordered collection with no duplicate elements. Basic uses include membership testing and eliminating duplicate entries. Set objects also support mathematical operations like union, intersection, difference and symmetric difference.

We don't want to implement an ordered set completely because we don't prefer one VIP customer over another or one non-VIP customer over another. If you are interested in a fully functional ordered set, you can check the ordered sorted container Python library.[7]

The problem then boils down to the implementation of the *__iter__* method which dictates the behavior of iteration. Interestingly, the *SymPy* developers faced a similar concern like ours. They want to implement the rational number set and allow callers to iterate over the set in a specific way. Why? Recall that a rational number is any number that can be represented as a fraction. For example, $\frac{1}{2}, \frac{3}{5}$ are both rational numbers while π, the ratio of a circle's circumference to its diameter, is not. The rational number set is also infinitely large. Iterating over such an infinite set exhaustively and reasonably is their concern.

The source code is in the *sympy.sets.fancysets.Rationals* class as shown in code snippet 1.14.

```
def __iter__(self):
    from sympy.core.numbers import igcd, Rational  # comment 1
    yield S.Zero
    yield S.One
    yield S.NegativeOne
    d = 2
    while True:
        for n in range(d):
```

```
            if igcd(n, d) == 1:   # comment 2
                yield Rational(n, d)
                yield Rational(d, n)
                yield Rational(-n, d)
                yield Rational(-d, n)
        d += 1
```

CODE 1.14   Generate all rational numbers systematically.

In the line denoted with the first comment, they used a function called *igcd()* to determine whether two numbers are relatively prime. The *Rational* class is used to build a rational number. Two rational numbers are essentially the same if one can be reduced to another. For example, $\frac{1}{2}$ is essentially equivalent to $\frac{23}{46}$. Several Singleton objects are being yielded in the following lines first. There is only one 0, one positive 1 and one negative 1, etc.

Then the iteration is dictated by increasing a value *d*, while finding all the possible combinations of the pair (n, d), where *n* is smaller than *d* and relatively prime to it.

Notice that the __iter__ method can yield rational numbers indefinitely, which gives you an idea why protocols are important to write efficient code. The code doesn't need to be honest if it does what it is supposed to do faithfully, according to the protocol. For example, you can pass a handler to users to iterate over a large amount of data records from a database. You don't want to query so much data beforehand because it is going to be a disaster memory-wise and time-wise. What you can do is to return a small amount of data for the user to use, maintain a cursor and defer additional queries until needed. The amortized cost will be low.

Let's give it a try to check the pattern. I am examining the first 20 results in code snippet 1.15.

```
for idx, val in enumerate(sympy.Rationals):
    if idx < 20:
        print(val)
    else:
        break
# 0
# 1
# -1
# 1/2
# 2
# -1/2
# -2
# 1/3
# 3
# -1/3
# -3
# 2/3
```

```
#  3/2
#  -2/3
#  -3/2
#  1/4
#  4
#  -1/4
#  -4
#  3/4
```

CODE 1.15   Use the *Rationals* class to generate first 20 rational numbers.

Time to go back to our *CustomerStruct* case. We also need to slightly modify the *Customer* class to initiate them with an *is _ vip* argument (snippet 1.16).

```
class Customer:
    def __init__(self, ..., is_vip: bool)
    self.is_vip = is_vip


class CustomerStruct:
    def __init__(self, customer_set: set):
        self.customer_set = customer_set

    def __iter__(self):
        for customer in self.customer_set:
            if customer.is_vip:
                yield customer
        for customer in self.customer_set:
            if not customer.is_vip:
                yield customer
```

CODE 1.16   Iterate through VIP customers first.

The drawback of this approach is that we will have to loop the *customer _ set* twice. Well, there is no free lunch. Better solutions so exist but you get the point.

ATTRIBUTES, FUNCTION OR DICTIONARY?

The flexibility of Python is one of its main strengths, as well as a timed bomb if used improperly. In the last section, let's think about a case where we have different approaches to solve the same problem, although some approaches seem intuitively weird.

A defined instance attribute can be found in the __*dict*__ dictionary that the instance maintains. Code snippet 1.17 is an example.

```
class Customer:
    def __init__(self, is_vip: bool):
        self.is_vip = is_vip
print(Customer(True).__dict__)
```

```
# {'is_vip': True}
```

CODE 1.17   Check a class' __dict__ attribute.

It looks like the attribute retrieval is merely a *get()* call on the __dict__ attribute.

Shall we manipulate the instance's attribute dictionary directly whenever an attribute is not found? Say you want to make room for flexibility. If a code user asks for an attribute *is _ VIP* rather than *is _ vip*, you still want to return the *is _ vip* attribute value and log a warning message rather than throwing out an error. Can we do that?

Some readers may know that behind the scenes, there is a beginner-unfriendly concept called descriptor for managed attribute lookup, storage and manipulation. We will cover it in the next chapter, together with the attribute lookup order.

Suppose that you follow the attribute lookup order and there is no attribute called *is _ VIP* anywhere, not the instance, not in the class *Customer* and all its parent classes. Python has a built-in special method called __getattr__ *()* to handle this safely. We can customize it to handle the error gracefully.

> In fact, the attribute access logic first goes through the __getattribute__ *()* dunder method. It is called regardless of whether the attribute exists first, and it is called before __getattr__ *()*, which serves as the last resort of failed attribute retrieval attempt.

The logic in code snippet 1.18 is that whenever an attribute that contains the string *vip* is requested, we return the *is _ vip* value.

```
# class Customer:
def __getattr__(self, attr_name: str):
    if "vip" in attr_name.lower():
        return self.is_vip
    else:
        raise AttributeError(attr_name)
```

CODE 1.18   Allow minor typo to work while retrieving VIP status.

This works.

The __getattr__ *()* is a catch-all fallback method as the last resolution. If there is no user-defined __getattr__ *()* method, the default behavior is just to raise an *AttributeError* exception.

The lesson here is that the *instance.attribute* syntax is largely *implemented* as a dictionary lookup. Can we do it the other way around? Can we fake a dictionary lookup process by something else, like a function call, etc.? Sure.

SymPy has an example exactly for this. In *SymPy*, there is a class called *Transform* that represents a mathematical transformation. Since high school, we know this is naturally represented as a function. However, in *SymPy*, it is abstractly represented by a custom class, partially implementing the *Mapping* protocol. Code snippet 1.19 is the key part of it.

```
class Transform:
    """
    documentation is omitted for the lack of space.
    """
    def __init__(self, transform, filter=lambda x: True):
        self._transform = transform
        self._filter = filter

    def __contains__(self, item):
        return self._filter(item)

    def __getitem__(self, key):
        if self._filter(key):
            return self._transform(key)
        else:
            raise KeyError(key)

    def get(self, item, default=None):
        if item in self:
            return self[item]
        else:
            return default
```

CODE 1.19 *Transform* is implemented as a map.

The *__getitem__ (key)* method is behind the *instance[key]* syntax, which is a dictionary lookup. However, it is then implemented as a function call by passing the *key* to the *_transform()* function, which is then used to initialize a *Transform* instance.

An instance of the *Transform* class is initiated with two functions, *transform* and *filter*. The transform function is used to transform an input, while the filter function is used to filter the input to indicate whether the transformation applies to the input or not.

We can build a *Transform* instance that only squares even numbers as shown in code snippet 1.20.

```
from sympy.core.rules import Transform
square_even = Transform(transform = lambda x: x**2, filter =
lambda x: x%2 == 0)


3 in square_even
# False

square_even[4]
# 16
```

CODE 1.20 A *Transform* that only squares even numbers.

Visually, *square _ even[4]* can also be interpreted as an array indexing: we want the fifth element in the list *square _ even*. However, *__getitem__ ()* for Mapping protocol has a signature of *__getitem__ (self, key)* while *__getitem__ ()* for Sequence protocol has a signature of *__getitem__ (self, index)*. Clearly, we are sticking to the Mapping protocol here.

A *square _ even* object behaves *like* a dictionary, but not exactly. For example, it doesn't have a *values* attribute, and you can't loop through its members. We cherrypicked what we need from the *Mapping* protocol and built our own class.

Well, a Python function itself is natively a mapping. Why don't we write a function like *square _ even(4)* directly? We surely can. We can implement the *__call__* dunder method for the *Transform* class to make an instance behave like a function as shown in code snippet 1.21.

```
class Transform:
    # omitted for the lack of space
    def __call__(self, val):
        if self._filter(val):
            return self._transform(val)
        return ValueError(val)
```

CODE 1.21   Add *__call__ ()* method to the *Transform* class.

By implementing the *__call__ ()* method, we are essentially adhering to the Callable protocol. Anything can *behave like* a function, if it implements an *__call__ ()* dunder method. Download a copy of the *SymPy* source code, manipulate the *Transform* class and give it a try.

At this moment, we have seen three different approaches to do something similar: through attribute accessing, dictionary-like lookup or function call. Which should we choose? The answer depends on the context and the actual implication of the scenario.

Take the *is _ vip* attribute as an obvious example, we can implement a dictionary look-up directly to enable syntax like *customer["is _ vip"]*. We can handle the missing key using the *__missing__ ()* dunder method, the fallback resolution counterpart of *__getattr__ ()*, for a dictionary-like data structure. However, it doesn't make sense because your colleagues are not supposed to *look for* the VIP status of a customer. They know it *must* be there. The look-up syntax creates an illusion that there may be some other keys to look up for, which there aren't.

Similarly, there is a justification for the *Transform* example. The *Mapping-like* modeling enables a correspondence between mathematical concepts and Python syntaxes. For example, in mathematics, we say the domain of a function or transformation is the set of all values on which a function is defined. Syntax in code snippet 1.22 is Pythonic and easy to understand: it is asking whether the number 3 is in the domain of our transformation.

Using function calls, we must pass 3 to the function and catch a *ValueError* exception, which is not intuitive: you may need to implement an error called *ValueNotInDomain* and your code users must know how to handle it. The *in* syntax is much more elegant.

```
3 in square_even
# False
```

CODE 1.22   Checking whether 3 is in the domain of *square _ even*.

There are other factors to consider as well. For example, function calls can accept more than one argument while attribute accessing, and dictionary look-up only accept one.

To quote Spider-Man: with great flexibility comes great responsibility. After all, we are all adults.

SUMMARY

In this chapter, we see that the Python data model is the core of the language and dictates the behavior of all kinds of objects. Python objects can be treated as realizations of protocols, with a huge level of freedom at the implementation level. We only touched the tip of the iceberg here. I encourage you to explore the usage of Python's data model in your favorite projects and see how they are used.

The next chapter will continue the path with a focus on user-defined classes. We will talk about the descriptor protocol that we skipped in this chapter; the class life cycles and some *practical* metaclass usages.

NOTES

1 If you find the first code sample difficult for you, this book may be too advanced for you.
2 https://docs.python.org/3/reference/datamodel.html
3 https://github.com/sympy/sympy/issues/20796
4 https://github.com/sympy/sympy/pull/20801
5 https://docs.python.org/3/library/collections.abc.html#module-collections.abc
6 https://sangmoonoh.medium.com/
7 https://grantjenks.com/docs/sortedcontainers/

## CHAPTER 2

Selected Topics of Python Classes

INTRODUCTION

I choose these two topics because they are often deemed as solutions that you will be looking for problems to apply on. However, normal Python users don't use them often.

In fact, a lot of Python built-in behaviors and functionalities from standard library are implemented using the descriptor protocol. The famous web framework Django uses metaclass to customize model classes. We will look at another example other than Django though, as every talk on metaclasses already used it.

This chapter is going to be fun. Let's dive in.

DESCRIPTORS AND ATTRIBUTE LOOKUP ORDER

First thing first, from previous chapter, we have two cliffhangers: descriptor and attribute lookup order. In fact, it is impossible to talk about attribute lookup order without introducing descriptor, as attributes managed by descriptors are kind of special.

Descriptor Demystified

A descriptor is just a class that implements *at least* one of the following three dunder methods. Sorry that I am introducing the concepts first, but I promise it is going to be smooth and easy.

1. `__get__(self, obj, type=None)→ value`

2. `__set__(self, obj, value) → None`

3. `__delete__(self, obj) → None`

That's it. Let's define a descriptor in code snippet 2.1.

DOI: 10.1201/9781003316909-3

```
class Answer:
    def __get__(self, obj, objtype):
        return 42
```

CODE 2.1   A simple Python descriptor called *Answer*.

The *Answer* class is a descriptor. To be more specific, it is a non-data descriptor, or a non-overriding descriptor. It means that this descriptor will be shadowed by attribute assignment. Instead, descriptors implementing __delete__() and __set__() are called data descriptors. They will not be shadowed by attribute assignment after initialization. We will see examples very soon.

Let's first check a simple use case of descriptor in code snippet 2.2.

```
class Answer:
    def __get__(self, obj, objtype):
        return 42


class Universe:
    answer = Answer() # comment 1

u = Universe()
print(u.answer) # 42
print(Universe.answer) # 42
```

CODE 2.2   Assign an *Answer* instance to an attribute.

answer is a class attribute. The instance *u* doesn't have an *answer* attribute, so it falls back to the class' attribute.

Next, we overwrite the instance's *answer* attribute in code snippet 2.3.

```
u = Universe()
print(u.__dict__) # {}
u.answer = 24
print(u.answer) # 24
print(u.__dict__) # {'answer': 24}
print(Universe.answer) # 42
```

CODE 2.3   Overwriting the *answer* descriptor of the class.

Code snippet 2.3 shows that *Answer* is a *non-data descriptor*: it doesn't *manage* data; it just gives back the data.

A non-data descriptor is a type of descriptor that only defines the __get__() method, but not the __set__() or __delete__() methods. When an attribute is accessed on an instance of a class that uses a non-data descriptor, the __get__() method of the descriptor is called, and the value returned by the method is used as the attribute value. However, attempts to set or delete the attribute will result in an AttributeError.

For non-data descriptors, the instance's __dict__ has higher priority. In another word, Python will prioritize the same-name key in instance's __dict__ before falling back to its class attribute.

Let's add a __set__ () dunder to the *Answer* class to make it a so-called *data descriptor*, also known as an *overriding descriptor*, and run the code again as code snippet 2.4.

```
class Answer:
    def __get__(self, obj, objtype):
        return 42
    def __set__(self, obj, value):
        obj.answer = value

class Universe:
    answer = Answer()

u = Universe()
print(u.answer) # 42

# The following line will cause an error:

u.answer = 24 # maximum recursion depth exceeded
```

CODE 2.4   Change *Answer* to a data descriptor.

At the end, we get a recursion error. To understand this error, we need to look at the meaning of the arguments for the __get__ () and __set__ () methods.

Take __get__ () for an example, *self* is the self-reference of the descriptor instance: the *answer* variable. The *obj* is the *instance* that the descriptor instance is assigned to. The *objtype* is the instance's type. Let's use code snippet 2.5 to show this explicitly.

```
# skipped the rest
    def __get__(self, obj, objtype):
        print(obj, objtype)
        return 42

u.answer
# <__main__.Universe object at 0x7f28856c22e0> <class '__main__.
Universe'>
Universe.answer
# None <class '__main__.Universe'>
```

CODE 2.5   The *obj* and *objtype* passed to the __get__ method.

If you invoke the descriptor from the class, there is no instance associated, so *obj* is None.

When we try to assign 24 to *u.answer*, the data descriptor's __set__ () method is invoked, which executes *obj.answer = 24*. However, *obj* is exactly the *Universe* instance *u*, and we are trying to assign to its *answer* attribute.

Wait a minute, that's exactly what we want at the beginning! We have an infinite recursion.

How to solve this issue?

The solution is to let descriptor manage and store our data. Let the *self,* the instance, store and manage everything, as shown in code snippet 2.6.

```
class Answer:
    def __get__(self, obj, type = None):
        return obj._answer
    def __set__(self, obj, value):
        obj._answer = value

class Universe:
    answer = Answer()
    def __init__(self, answer):
        self.answer = answer

u = Universe(42)
print(u.answer) # 42
u.answer = 24
print(u.answer) # 24
```

CODE 2.6   Let *Answer* descriptor hold the attributes.

The problem seems solved! If you are familiar with the *property()* decorator[1], you probably already recognized this pattern. In fact, *property()* is implemented using the descriptor.

This gives us enough knowledge to understand the full picture of instance attribute lookup order. In fact, we have demonstrated almost all relationships in his quote except the last one. Data descriptor preceding instance variables means that if an attribute has a *__get__()* method, call it instead of returning the *__dict__[attribute_name]* value.

Instance lookup scans through a chain of namespaces giving data descriptors the highest priority, followed by instance variables, then non-data descriptors, then class variables and lastly *__getattr__()* if it is provided.[2]

Code snippet 2.7 is one last example that shows the non-data descriptor does precede the class variable. Class A maintains a class attribute *answer* whose value is 24 while the instance has a non-data descriptor that says its *answer* attribute has a value of 42.

```
class Answer:
    def __get__(self, obj, type = None):
        return 42

class A:
    answer = 24
```

```
    _answer = Answer()
    def __init__(self):
        self.answer = A._answer

instance = A()
print(instance.answer) # 42
```

CODE 2.7   Non-data descriptor precedes class variable.

Next, let's pay attention to the elephant in the room: why we care about the lookup order and how our code can benefit from it.

Lazy Evaluation in Matplotlib

This example shows how descriptor can be used to postpone heavy work that may not be used, until it is really needed.

If you use Matplotlib to plot charts and want to allow readers to identify the values of your data points, you may consider adding ticks to your axis. Modifying the official Matplotlib example, Figures 2.1 and 2.2 are two charts that show the differences with or without ticks on the x-axis. They are generated with code snippet 2.8.

```
import numpy as np
import matplotlib.pyplot as plt
from matplotlib.ticker import AutoMinorLocator
t = np.arange(0.0, 100.0, 0.1)
s = np.sin(0.5 * np.pi * t) * np.exp(-t * 0.01)
fig, ax = plt.subplots()
ax.plot(t, s)
# ax.xaxis.set_minor_locator(AutoMinorLocator())
```

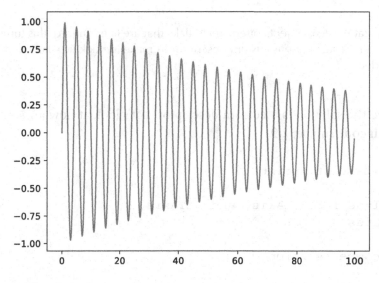

FIGURE 2.1   No ticks on x-axis.

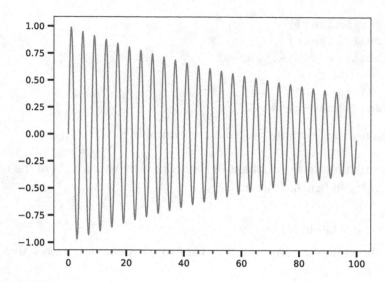

FIGURE 2.2   Ticks on x-axis.

```
# ax.tick_params(which='both', width=2)
# ax.tick_params(which='major', length=7)
# ax.tick_params(which='minor', length=4, color='r')
plt.show()
```

CODE 2.8   Python code that generates the `matplotlib` images with and without x-axis ticks.

Most of the time users don't need the ticks, therefore by default a chart doesn't have ticks. They should only be available when they are needed. In fact, creating ticks is kind of slow. Here, I quote the code comment in the *axis.py*[3] file.

> During initialization, Axis objects often create ticks that are later unused; this turns out to be a very slow step. Instead, use a custom descriptor to make the tick lists lazy and instantiate them as needed.

Well, we see the solution is a custom descriptor. Let's look at how an `Axis` object is initialized with code snippet 2.9.

```
class Axis(martist.Artist):
    """
    Base class for `.XAxis` and `.YAxis`.
    Attributes


    Other comments skipped


    majorTicks : list of `.Tick`
```

```
        The major ticks.
    minorTicks : list of `.Tick`
        The minor ticks.
    """

    # Code skipped

    # During initialization, Axis objects often create ticks that
are later
    # unused; this turns out to be a very slow step.  Instead, use
a custom
    # descriptor to make the tick lists lazy and instantiate them
as needed.
    majorTicks = _LazyTickList(major=True)
    minorTicks = _LazyTickList(major=False)
```

CODE 2.9   Axis object initialization.

The comments indicate that class attributes *majorTicks* and *minorTicks* are lists of *Tick*
objects. Code snippet 2.10 is the definition[4] of *_LazyTickList* descriptor.

```
class _LazyTickList:
    """
    A descriptor for lazy instantiation of tick lists.

    See comment above definition of the ``majorTicks`` and
``minorTicks``
    attributes.
    """

    def __init__(self, major):
        self._major = major


    def __get__(self, instance, cls):
        if instance is None:
            return self
        else:
            # instance._get_tick() can itself try to access the
majorTicks
            # attribute (e.g. in certain projection classes which
override
            # e.g. get_xaxis_text1_transform).  In order to avoid
infinite
            # recursion, first set the majorTicks on the instance
to an empty
            # list, then create the tick and append it.
            if self._major:
                instance.majorTicks = []
                tick = instance._get_tick(major=True)
                instance.majorTicks.append(tick)
```

```
            return instance.majorTicks
        else:
            instance.minorTicks = []
            tick = instance._get_tick(major=False)
            instance.minorTicks.append(tick)
            return instance.minorTicks
```

CODE 2.10   Definition of _LazyTickList

Here are 2 key discoveries:

1. _LazyTickList is a non-data descriptor, which means it can be shadowed.

2. The place where it is overwritten is in its own __get__ () method. It is self-destructive: once it gets called, it is terminated with its duty fulfilled.

Another interesting discovery is that we must set the *instance.majorTicks* or *instance. minorTicks* to an empty list first before calling the _get_tick() method. The reason is the same as ours earlier: to avoid infinite recursion.

> To avoid infinite recursion, first set the majorTicks on the instance to an empty list, then create the tick and append it.

By setting the ticks to descriptors, if a user never accesses the ticks, then they remain descriptors and no one will know. Once a user accesses the ticks or tries to set it to another set of *Tick* object, the descriptors will be overwritten, and they are gone forever.

There is a decorator, implemented as a class, in Python *functools* module: cached_ property. cached_property allows you to perform a calculation that takes long time for the first time you run a method, then set the result to the same name attribute. Next time you access the *method*, it is no longer a method, but a precomputed value.

Code snippet 2.11 is an example to compare the differences between *property* decorator and cached_property decorator.

```
import time
from functools import cached_property

class Calculator:

    @property
    def p_calculation(self):
        x = 0.3
        for i in range(1_000_000):
            x = 4 * x * (1-x)
        return x
```

```
    @cached_property
    def cp_calculation(self):
        x = 0.3
        for i in range(1_000_000):
            x = 4 * x * (1-x)
        return x

c = Calculator()
start = time.time()
for _ in range(10):
    c.p_calculation
end = time.time()
print(end - start) # about 1.28 seconds

start = time.time()
for _ in range(10):
    c.cp_calculation
end = time.time()
print(end - start) # about 0.13 seconds
```

CODE 2.11   Compare *property* and `cached_property` decorators.

Clearly, the cached version is much faster. However, suppose you *want* the instance to keep track of the value of *x*. Then you should stick with *property*. The following code snippet 2.12 will run faster but run it wrong.

```
class Calculator:

    def __init__(self, x):
        self.x = x

    @cached_property
    def cp_calculation(self):
        for i in range(1_000_000):
            self.x = 4 * self.x * (1-self.x)
        return self.x

c = Calculator(0.3)
for _ in range(10):
    print(c.cp_calculation) # always 0.9892353585201644
```

CODE 2.12   A case that `cached_property` doesn't work.

The idea of `_LazyTickList` is very similar to `cached_property`: the first access makes a fundamental change and does the heavy lifting. Everything that follows becomes standard.

METACLASS AND ITS USAGE IN ELASTICSEARCH DSL

In this section, we will dive into metaclasses, from the very basics. We will also take Elasticsearch domain-specific language (DSL) as an example to examine its usage in this open source project.

Understanding Metaclass Using Meta-Recipe

What is a metaclass in Python? A metaclass is a class that can create classes. As we discussed in Chapter 2, everything in Python is an object. To create an instance, we call the corresponding class. We can customize the creation of the instance by initializing it with different arguments. We can do some logic checking in the __init__ () method to ensure everything is good.

Similarly, sometimes we want code users to create their own *classes*, so they can create their own instances. We want to do *something* about their classes before they are used to create instances. For example, those classes need to be either *validated*, *enchanted* or *transformed*. This is where metaclass shines.

For most scenarios, we provide classes for other developers to use rather than allow them to build *enchanted* classes. This is why metaclass is often only *legitimately* used in libraries that allow users to build tools to achieve their own customized tasks. For other occasions, I think 99% of the time, you can achieve the same effect without using metaclass.

Here is a scenario.

You are the *head* of the kitchens of a big hotel. You don't cook, instead you manage the cooks and the operation of the kitchens.

Other cooks continuously create new recipes to satisfy guests' endless appetite. Every day, each meal is cooked according to its recipe for hundreds of times. You want to ensure that the foods are always safe and healthy.

According to the scenario, we have the corresponding relationship as shown in Figure 2.3.

Let's pay attention to the right two columns. A recipe is a template for creating foods. Their relationship is just like classes and instances. You as the head of kitchen need to own something called *Meta Recipe* to manage the creation of all possible recipes. In Python, this position in the hierarchy is reserved for metaclass.

To make this example more specific, let's say you want to make sure that all recipe ingredients don't contain eel. This is just a random example. I personally love eel a lot.

The code is presented in code snippet 2.13.

```python
class RecipeMeta(type):

    @classmethod
    def _ingredient_check(cls, ingredients:list):
        if 'eel' in ingredients:
            return False
        return True
```

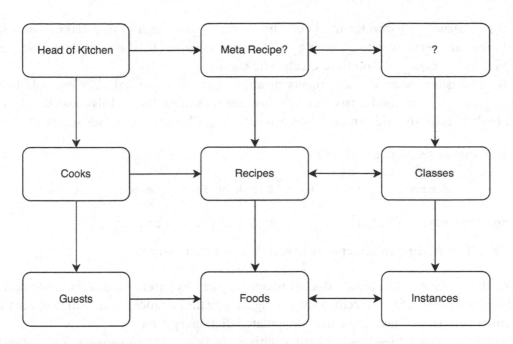

FIGURE 2.3 Head of kitchen entity relationship diagram.

```
def __new__(cls, class_name, bases, attrs):
        if "ingredients" not in attrs:
                raise Exception("Dish class must have
ingredients!")
        if not cls._ingredient_check(attrs['ingredients']):
                raise Exception("Eel is not allowed in the
ingredients!")
        return type(class_name, bases, attrs)


class ChickenStew(metaclass = RecipeMeta):
    ingredients = ('chicken',)


class SmokedEel(metaclass = RecipeMeta):
    ingredients = ('eel',)
```

CODE 2.13 The *RecipeMeta* metaclass

Run this snippet, you will get an error that the *definition* of *SmokedEel* raised an exception. It is very important that this happens in the class definition rather than instance creation. In real life, it corresponds to the process that you, as the head of kitchen, review a recipe proposal and you reject it. You don't need to see an *actual* plate of smoked eel to reject it.

Let's take a close look at the *RecipeMeta*. It is extending *type* which indicates that it is a metaclass. In Python, all metaclasses are children of *type*. The magic happens in the __new__() dunder method. The __new__() method of a class *creates* its instance and returns it to __init__() to initialize it. In the metaclass case, the metaclass' __new__() method creates the class.

To understand what the arguments mean, let's check a normal class example first. The __new__() method exists for every class, not only metaclasses. This class extends the *dict* built-in class and adds an underscore to every key. Check it out in code snippet 2.14.

```
class UnderScoreDict(dict):
    def __new__(cls, d):
        return {"_" + str(k):v for k,v in d.items()}

UnderScoreDict({"a":1, "b":2}) # {'_a': 1, '_b': 2}
```

CODE 2.14   Adding an underscore to each key of a dictionary.

First, the __new__() method doesn't necessarily call its parent's methods. Instead, the only requirement is for it to return something, ideally the instance, for initialization in the downstream. Here, I just create the manipulated dictionary directly.

Second, can we achieve the same thing with __init__()? The answer is Yes as shown in code snippet 2.15.

```
class UnderScoreDict(dict):
    def __init__(self, d):
        for k,v in d.items():
            self["_" + str(k)] =  v
```

CODE 2.15   Achieve the same effect without using metaclass.

The default __new__() method returns an empty dictionary to the __init__() method to initialize, and __init__() assigns the key-value pairs one by one.

In practice, there are situations where only __new__() can resolve. For example, you want to make sure there is only one instance in your program: the singleton design pattern, which you already saw in Chapter 2. Code snippet 2.16 creates a singleton.

```
class Singleton:
    _instance = None
    def __new__(cls, *args, **kwargs):
        if not cls._instance:
            cls._instance = object.__new__(cls, *args, **kwargs)
        return cls._instance
```

CODE 2.16   A *singleton* class always returns the same entity.

In this example, the class *Singleton* maintains a class variable _instance. Every time a new instance is created, the __new__() method checks whether this is the first time such an instance is created. If yes, create the instance, track it with the _instance variable, then return it. If not, just return the instance created earlier.

TABLE 2.1   Arguments of Metaclass' __new__() method

Argument Name	Meaning	Value
cls	the metaclass	`<class '__main__.RecipeMeta'>`
class_name	the name of the created class	`ChickenStew`
bases	the parents of the created class	`()`
attrs	attribute dictionary of the created class	`{'__module__': '__main__', '__qualname__': 'ChickenStew', 'ingredients': ('chicken',)}`

This is not achievable with __*init*__ () as it is not in charge of instance creation. In fact, __*new*__ () can do everything that __*init*__ () can do, but not vice versa. Well, using __*init*__ () allows users to focus on the business logic, as the majority of the time users don't care about the creation of the instance.

Now, move on to the metaclass cases. Our example is a little different as we are customizing the creation of a class. The __*new*__ () method takes four arguments, which I lay out in a table (Table 2.1).

If you inherent the *ChickenStew* class to create something like *SpanishChickenStew*, then *ChickenStew* should appear in the *bases*. There is a pitfall here which we will discuss very soon.

The argument `class_name` is a string. What we get out of the metaclass calling is a class. Who does the magic? It is the `type(class_name, bases, attrs)` that is responsible for such construction.

`type()` can take either 1 or 3 arguments. The common one-argument usage returns the type of an object. However, when feeding 3 arguments, it can create arbitrary classes. Code snippet 2.17 provides an example.

```
class_name = "Duck"
quack = lambda x: "Quack"
class Bird:
    pass

Duck = type(class_name, (Bird,), {'quack':quack})

duck = Duck()
print(duck.quack()) # Quack
duck.__class__.mro() # [__main__.Duck, __main__.Bird, object]
```

CODE 2.17   Dynamic class creation with `type()`.

I created a *Duck* class without writing the normal class definition. Instead, I created it by passing its class name, its parent *Bird* and a `quack()` lambda function to the `type()` function.

This is amazing and super powerful.

However, there is one last issue with this example. If you did create a subclass of *ChickenStew* with eel in its ingredient, the check fails to work. The following code snippet 2.18 works fine, by passing the checking.

```
class SpanishChickenStew(ChickenStew):
    ingredients = ('eel',)
```

CODE 2.18   Subclasses don't inherit metaclass.

Without explicitly specifying the metaclass, the subclasses don't *inherit* the metaclass. However, there is a workaround. The *type(class_name, bases, attrs)* also contains two stages, the *type.__new__(cls_type, class_name, bases, attrs)* and *type.__init__(cls, class_name, bases, attrs)*. If we don't overwrite the *cls_type* variable in the *type.__new__()* function, the returned class has a default metaclass: *type*, rather than *RecipeMeta*.

Code snippet 2.19 shows the fix.

```
def __new__(cls, class_name, bases, attrs):
        if "ingredients" not in attrs:
            raise Exception("Dish class must have ingredients!")
        if not cls._ingredient_check(attrs['ingredients']):
            raise Exception("Eel is not allowed in the
ingredients!")
        return type.__new__(cls, class_name, bases, attrs)
```

CODE 2.19   The fix of metaclass' inheritance.

Now, no one can smuggle eel to a Chicken recipe. Applying *type()* on *SpanishChickenStew* will return its metaclass as in code snippet 2.20.

```
type(SpanishChickenStew)
# __main__.RecipeMeta
```

CODE 2.20   The class type works properly.

Finally, before moving on to the Elasticsearch DSL example, I want to summarize the definitions of *type* used in this section. I know it is often confusing (Table 2.2).

There are some other special treatments of *type* in Python like it is its own instance, but the four usages above are the most common ones.

TABLE 2.2   Common Usage of *type* in Python

Usage	Meaning	Example
type(instance)	returns the class/type of the instance	`type(12) # <class 'int'>`
type(class)	returns the metaclass of the class	`type(dict) # <class 'type'>`
type	as a metaclass that all metaclasses inherent	`class RecipeMeta(type):` `    pass`
type(class_name, bases, attributes)	returns a class that is dynamically created	`Duck = type(class_name, (Bird,),` `{'quack':quack})`

Use Metaclass to Model Documents in Elasticsearch DSL

The open source project we are going to study is called elasticsearch-dsl-py.[5] It provides easy-to-use syntax to manipulate queries and performs object-document mapping out of the box.

Here is a quick introduction of Elasticsearch. Elasticsearch is a search engine based on the Lucene library. It provides a full-text search engine with an HTTP web interface and schema-free JSON documents. Elasticsearch is closer to MongoDB than PostgreSQL. It stores records as documents. Here is a concept mapping between Elasticsearch and SQL-like databases. This does require that you have some basic knowledge of SQL or both (Table 2.3).

To simplify the idea, I will refer to the example used in elasticsearch-dsl-py's documentation, you can imagine the following json object is a *document*, and you can save it and other similar objects to an *index* called blog. The document has five *fields*: `author, title, publish_date, tags` and body, as shown in code snippet 2.20.

```
{
    "author": "Richard. W",
    "title": "Rule of Apes",
    "body": "a long long body.",
    "published_date": "2021-03-21",
    "tags": ["sci-fi", "thriller"]
}
```

CODE 2.20   A sample *document* in the blog *index*.

After saving this document to Elasticsearch, you can search for it by text. You can use "apes" or "Richard" as keywords to search in the title field or in the author field. Elasticsearch will use *analyzers* to analyze different fields. For example, a good text analyzer will find *apes* for you even if you typed *ape*, etc.

What's a domain-specific language (DSL)? A domain-specific language is a programming language that is designed to solve problems in a specific domain. They are not for general purposes. For example, SQL is for relational database operation. HTML is only for frontend development. LaTeX is only for document typesetting. Elasticsearch DSL is not really a language but a library that can, I quote, help with writing and running queries against Elasticsearch. It provides a more convenient and idiomatic way to write and manipulate queries.

TABLE 2.3   Concepts Matching in Elasticsearch and SQL-Like Databases

Elasticsearch Concepts	SQL Concepts
Index	Table
Document	Row
Field	Column
None	Schema

How so? Let's look at the official example of Elasticsearch DSL. Let's say you want to save an *article* object and save it to the *blog* index. To run this example, you need to set up an Elasticsearch instance locally. I provided the how-to in the appendix of this chapter.

First, let's create an *Article* class that represents an article with code snippet 2.21.

```python
from datetime import datetime
from elasticsearch_dsl import Document, Date, Integer, Keyword,
Text, connections
connections.create_connection(hosts=['localhost'], port=9200)


class Article(Document):
    title = Text(analyzer='snowball', fields={'raw': Keyword()})
    body = Text(analyzer='snowball')
    tags = Keyword()
    published_from = Date()
    lines = Integer()

    class Index:
        name = 'blog'
        settings = {
            "number_of_shards": 2,
        }

    def save(self, ** kwargs):
        self.lines = len(self.body.split())
        return super(Article, self).save(** kwargs)

    def is_published(self):
        return datetime.now() > self.published_from


Article.init()
```

CODE 2.21 Create the *Article* class.

Then, we can create a concrete article and save it with code snippet 2.22.

```python
article = Article(meta={'id': 45},
                  title='Hello world!',
                  tags=['real'],
                  body=''' long text that spawns multiple lines
''',
                  published_from=datetime.now())
article.save()
```

CODE 2.22 Create an article instance.

If you have experience working with ORM (object-relational mapping), you probably already recognized that this is very similar to the idea of ORM. Instead of using an object to represent a *row*, we use an object to represent a *document*, which is Elasticsearch's row.

We defined the *Article* class as a subclass of the *Document* class. The Article class doesn't have an *init ()* method defined and the *article* instance doesn't have a *save ()* method defined. Like our own example, there is a class factory, a metaclass that is responsible for *enchanting* the classes user defined.

Let's walk through code snippet 2.23 to see where *init ()* is defined for a new class. You are well-equipped to explore other facets on your own.

```
class Document(ObjectBase, metaclass=IndexMeta):
    """
    Model-like class for persisting documents in elasticsearch.
    """
    @classmethod
    def init(cls, index=None, using=None):
        """
        Create the index and populate the mappings in
elasticsearch.
        """
        i = cls._index
        if index:
            i = i.clone(name=index)
        i.save(using=using)
```

CODE 2.23   The definition of *init ()* of *Document* class.

The *Document* class has a metaclass *IndexMeta*. *init ()* is a classmethod in which a class' *_index* attribute calls its own *clone()* and *save()* methods.

The inline comment is accurate, let's find out how *_index* is created since we didn't create this attribute. Let's look at the *IndexMeta* metaclass, which is copied to code snippet 2.24.

```
class IndexMeta(DocumentMeta):
    # global flag to guard us from associating an Index with the
base Document
    # class, only user defined subclasses should have an _index
attr
    _document_initialized = False

    def __new__(cls, name, bases, attrs):
        new_cls = super().__new__(cls, name, bases, attrs)
        if cls._document_initialized:
            index_opts = attrs.pop("Index", None)
            index = cls.construct_index(index_opts, bases)
            new_cls._index = index
```

```
            index.document(new_cls)
        cls._document_initialized = True
        return new_cls


    @classmethod
    def construct_index(cls, opts, bases):
        if opts is None:
            for b in bases:
                if hasattr(b, "_index"):
                    return b._index

            # Set None as Index name so it will set _all while
making the query
            return Index(name=None)

        i = Index(getattr(opts, "name", "*"), using=getattr(opts,
"using", "default"))
        i.settings(**getattr(opts, "settings", {}))
        i.aliases(**getattr(opts, "aliases", {}))
        for a in getattr(opts, "analyzers", ()):
            i.analyzer(a)
        return i
```

CODE 2.24 *IndexMeta* metaclass definition.

In the __*new*__ *()* method, we see that `index_opts` is defined by popping *Index* out of the attributes dictionary. Where is the *Index*? It is in our own definition of *Article* as shown in code snippet 2.25. You can try to change its class name and you will see the article won't save to the *blog* index.

```
class Index:
    name = 'blog'
    settings = {
        "number_of_shards": 2,
    }
```

CODE 2.25 The *Index* class is defined inside the *Article* class.

If we don't define such a class, the document Article will be saved to a default *None* index. Here we define an index whose name is *blog*, which is equivalent to creating a table whose name is blog in a relational database.

Next, the `construct_index()` class method creates an *Index* object. The *Index* object configures the name and the settings of an index as shown in code snippet 2.26.

```
i = Index(getattr(opts, "name", "*"), using=getattr(opts, "using",
"default"))
```

CODE 2.26 Index creation in the `construct_index()` classmethod.

Next, the newly created index object is assigned to the new class' _index attribute.

If you are interested, you can dive into the *Index* class in the index.py[6] file.

When everything is done, the new_class is passed back to the user with all the messy preparation under the rug. There are many tedious details here and there. Everything is taken care of by metaclass, rather than user-defined classes. The users don't need to worry about which API to call to create an index, etc. All the users care about are the actual structure of an article.

To summarize, Figure 2.4 compares the patterns with and without metaclass.

How to justify the usage of metaclass? Suppose there is a system with a high level of internal complexity. The system can be a database, a search engine or just a large system another team built. Now you need to set rules for users to interact with such a complicated system. Every class they created needs to be in a very good standing. You have two options to ensure the class is compatible, healthy and well-functioning.

1. Option 1, you create a metaclass to talk to the system and the class, to make sure that both sides are happy, and the class is solid since inception.

2. Option 2, you throw 100 terms for the class creator to follow and hope there is no mistake.

This is where metaclass really shines. The conservation of complexity is like the conservation of energy: if you can't reduce complexity anymore, you had better move it to somewhere safe.

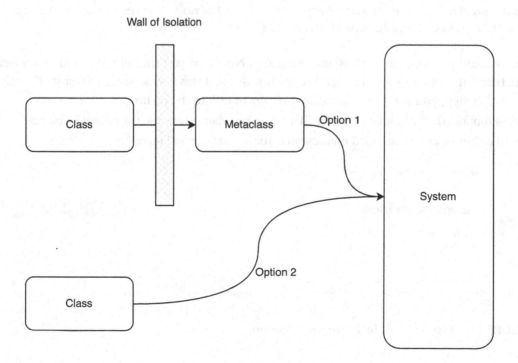

FIGURE 2.4   Patterns with and without metaclass.

SUMMARY

It is fascinating that the descriptor protocol is responsible for so many features and characteristics of Python classes. We went through the basic anatomy of descriptors and showed examples in the Matplotlib library and built-in modules.

Metaclass provides a *separation of concerns* in programming. It enables powerful class customization and creation in the class definition time, rather than instance creation time. This way, end users can focus on their own object modeling or other business concerns.

APPENDIX

Here is a quick how-to to set up an Elasticsearch instance running locally. I have tested it on a Mac machine with an M1 chip. With minor tweaks, it should work for other operating systems easily.

Step 1: Install Docker if you don't have it on your system. Go to the docker desktop[7] page, it should install the right version based on your operating system.

Step 2: Open a terminal and pull the docker image by running the command in code sample 2.27.

```
docker pull docker.elastic.co/elasticsearch/elasticsearch:8.5.3
```

CODE 2.27   Obtain the Elasticsearch image.

Step 3: Run the following command to start an `Elasticsearch` container with the security feature disabled, as shown in code sample 2.28.

```
docker run --rm -p 9200:9200 -p 9300:9300 -e "xpack.security.
enabled=false" -e "discovery.type=single-node" docker.elastic.co/
elasticsearch/elasticsearch:8.5.3
```

This should get your docker instance running. Note that you should never start a service like this if it is open to the internet. We are just doing it this way so you can test stuff easily.

At this step, you can use *elasticsearch-dsl-py* to talk to the instance.

Step 4 (optional): If you want to have a GUI to see how data is saved in the instance, you can install a chrome extension called Elasticsearch Tools[8] as shown in Figure 2.5.

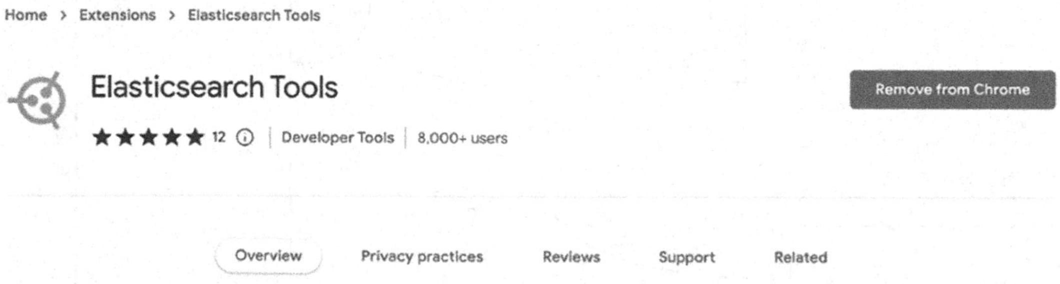

Home > Extensions > Elasticsearch Tools

Elasticsearch Tools

★★★★★ 12 ⓘ | Developer Tools | 8,000+ users

Remove from Chrome

Overview   Privacy practices   Reviews   Support   Related

FIGURE 2.5   Elasticsearch Tool Chrome extension.

I personally love to use it as it is very light and intuitive. Kibana[9] is the default choice for Elasticsearch tech stack that you can explore too.

NOTES

1 https://docs.python.org/3/library/functions.html#property
2 https://docs.python.org/3/howto/descriptor.html
3 https://github.com/matplotlib/matplotlib/blob/main/lib/matplotlib/axis.py#L572
4 https://github.com/matplotlib/matplotlib/blob/main/lib/matplotlib/axis.py#L560
5 https://github.com/elastic/elasticsearch-dsl-py
6 https://github.com/elastic/elasticsearch-dsl-py/blob/main/elasticsearch_dsl/index.py
7 https://www.docker.com/products/docker-desktop/
8 https://chrome.google.com/webstore/detail/elasticsearch-tools/aombbfhbleaidjmbahldfbajjmg-kgojl?hl=en
9 https://www.elastic.co/kibana/

## CHAPTER 3

Concurrency in Python

CONCURRENCY FROM A TOP-DOWN PERSPECTIVE

Imagine that you and your friends are waiting in a restaurant. You ordered French fries, roast chicken, beef stew and some salads. After about 15 minutes, all the food is ready. You are very happy.

From your perspective, the cooking of the food *happens* at the same time. In other words, they happen concurrently. You, as a diner, don't care about what happens in the kitchen. What you care about is that you can enjoy the French fries and the beef stew at the same time.

Being concurrent is a behavioral property of an application or a system. It is something we observe from the outside of a system. Having a *concurrent* kitchen doesn't say anything about the actual cooking of the food. There is something that I call an observation barrier that hides the actual *implementation* of concurrency (Figure 3.1).

Now, let's shift the perspective to the kitchen side. Suppose the four dishes require the following task and time to complete as shown in Table 3.1.

If there is only one cook in the kitchen and she must prepare the four dishes by herself, what would she do?

If she does each task sequentially, the total time is 29 minutes, which is unacceptable for the diners. However, anyone who has ever cooked will do something like the following.

First, she needs to put the pre-prepared chicken in the oven and start stewing the beef as they both take time. Setting timers is a good idea. Then, she prepares the salad as it is cold anyway. Lastly, she needs to fry the potato stripes and closely monitor it as it is easy to get under-fried or over-fried. French fries are better served hot, so we do it at the end. During the cooking process, it is safe to check the chicken and beef to make sure they are good until the timers ring.

In the time domain, the cooking tasks look like Figure 3.2.

The tasks marked with white are tasks that only need occasional attention. The shaded tasks are attention-exhausting. Remember, there is only one cook in the kitchen, but she can prepare these four dishes just fine.

DOI: 10.1201/9781003316909-4

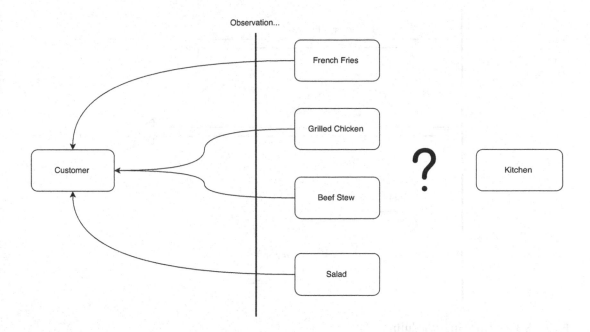

FIGURE 3.1 Kitchen concurrency from the customers' perspective.

TABLE 3.1 Dishes and Their Preparing Efforts

Dish Name	Task	Effort	Mostly Waiting?
French Fries	Fry the pre-cut potato	2 minutes	No
Roast Chicken	Roast the chicken	10 minutes	Yes
Beef Stew	Heat the pre-prepared beef	14 minutes	Yes
Salad	Cut vegetables and add dressing	3 minutes	No

Why? At any specific moment, she is only *busy* doing one thing and one thing only. She may be *doing* two or even more things but cooking the chicken and beef doesn't require much attention: she is mostly waiting for the timer to ring or occasionally checking. In short, she is *not busy* cooking two dishes simultaneously at any moment.

In the cook's eyes, being concurrent is a structural property that different components of a task or different sub-tasks, if you consider serving the diner as a super-task, can be performed *out of order* or in parallel, to still obtain the same deterministic results.

Note that there are two significant differences between the blue cooking tasks and red cooking tasks.

1. First, blue tasks are done in parallel, which means the two dishes do have overlapping cooking time. The red ones don't.

2. Second, blue tasks are not limited by the cook's energy, you can just wait. The red ones require the cook's full attention. Therefore, the red ones can only be prepared sequentially as there is only one cook.

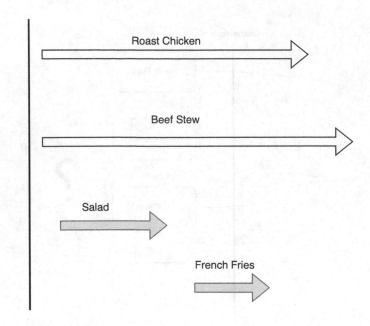

FIGURE 3.2 Cooking scheduling.

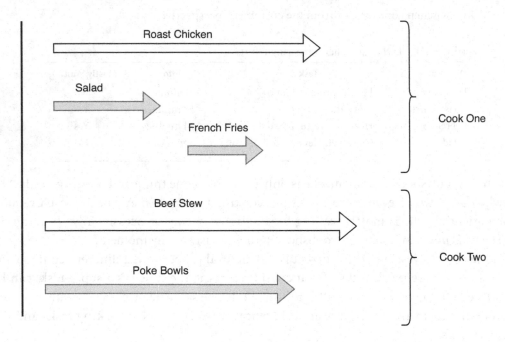

FIGURE 3.3 Two cooks case.

Things will become harder if diners also order three poke bowls, which each takes 4 minutes to prepare. In that case, the kitchen really needs one more cook (Figure 3.3).

With more cooking/processing power, even attention-exhausting tasks can be paralleled. Note that the diners don't need to know how many cooks are in the kitchen if their requests are met concurrently.

Operating System and Concurrency

Next, we are ready to combine the restaurant example with our operating system knowledge. If you are reading this book on your computer, the relationship between the diners and the kitchen is just like the relationship between you and your computer, more specifically, the operating system. Just as the diners order food and the kitchen prepares it, we ask the operating systems to do various tasks for us. Just as there are a lot of things going on in the kitchen that diners don't know or don't care about, there are also a lot of things going on in the operating system that we end-users don't care about.

Table 3.2 lays out the analogy between these two relationships. Remember, we are still discussing the general programming scenario. In CPython, there are some differences that we will discuss very soon.

Let's look at the similarities and differences between a CPU and a cook. They are both the heavy lifters of actual tasks. For a single-core CPU, there is no real parallelism as it can only perform one task at a time. A CPU will switch between tasks to provide an illusion that it does several things simultaneously. However, for a cook, roasting chicken and stewing beef can somehow be considered *real* parallelism still.

So why are there two modellings for tasks: processes and threads? What's the difference?

Simply put, threads can be treated as lightweight processes *within* a process with shared resources, smaller footprint and less creation overhead.

Processes are heavy. The operating system keeps track of resources a process uses like the file descriptor, the memory location and the port number, etc. By creating lightweight threads in a process, they can share some resources like the shared memory and use them. This is obviously powerful as well as dangerous. Writing the so-called multithreading code is considered difficult even for experienced developers.

Table 3.3 summarizes the key differences between process and thread.

TABLE 3.2   Compare the User-Operating Relationship with the Diner-Kitchen Relationship

User-Operating System Scenario	Diner-Kitchen Scenario
User	Diner
Operating system	Kitchen
CPU	Cook
Processes and threads	Dish cooking tasks

TABLE 3.3   Key Differences between Process and Thread

Perspective	Process	Thread
Independency	Processes are considered independent by the Operating system	Threads in the same process are considered dependent
Memory Sharing	Processes have different memory space	Threads in the same process can share memory
Data and Code sharing	Processes have independent data and code segments.	Threads in the same process share the same data segment, code segment, files, etc.
Overhead	Processes take longer time to create, terminate, etc.	Threads require less time to create, terminate, etc.

In general, different threads in a process *can* run in parallel. If the operating system has access to multiple CPUs, it can assign different threads to different CPUs. For simplicity, we are not considering multiple-core CPUs and other varieties.

The question now is how does the operating system achieve concurrency? The answer can be answered by following a set of Yes-No questions.

1. Is there real parallelism involved? Parallelism means that more than one CPU is processing tasks.

   a. If Yes, at what level?

      i. Process level: multiprocessing

      ii. Thread level: multithreading

   b. If No, a single thread can also achieve concurrency, which will be covered in the next chapter. Concurrency doesn't need to be achieved through parallelization. It heavily depends on the nature of the task.

In the rest of this chapter, we cover the first two cases. The first case is multiprocessing. See Figure 3.4 for the visualization: three processes run on three different CPUs.

The second case is Multithreading. We can also combine multiprocessing and multithreading. This is a common pattern in scientific computing.

As shown in Figure 3.5, process 1 has 3 threads that are running in parallel on three different CPUs. Process 2 only has 1 thread, running on another CPU.

It is important to mention the idea of thread safety a little bit. An operation/function is thread safe if it can work properly and reliably in a multithreading environment. For general programming, since threads can share resources like variables, database connections, etc., there may be race conditions that two or more threads try to manipulate the same shared objects. Imagine the cooking scenario. If two chefs are using a knife at the same time without *properly* cleaning it, a guest may have a serious food allergy. And, of course, two chefs cannot use a knife at the *exact* same time.

Everything seems nice so far. However, the existence of GIL in Python makes Python a little bit special.

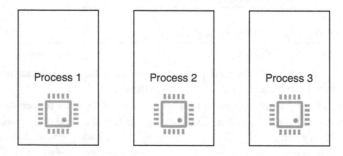

FIGURE 3.4   Multiprocessing for three processes on three CPUs.

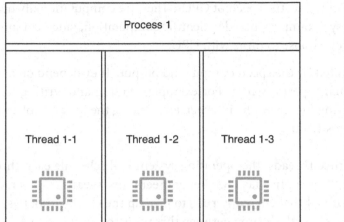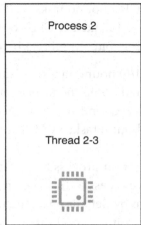

FIGURE 3.5   A process *can* have multiple threads.

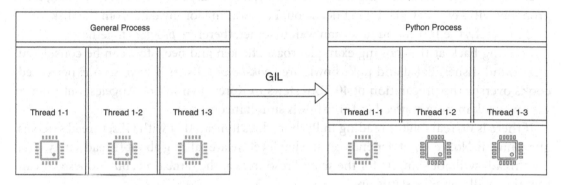

FIGURE 3.6   GIL limits Python's multithreading to fully utilize multiple CPUs.

Introducing Global Interpreter Lock (GIL)

In the most widely used Python implementation CPython, GIL ensures that a Python process, at any time, can only have one *running* thread. It means that even if there are multiple threads in a single Python process, only one of them can run at a time.

Figure 3.6 shows that threads 1-1, 1-2 and 1-3 *compete* for one CPU although there are two other idle CPUs marked as shaded.

GIL is a result of history. In the old days, computers only had one CPU, and a CPU only had one core. Having GIL makes single-thread code run quickly and safely. It also makes writing C extensions for Python much easier, which is considered one reason for the booming of the Python ecosystem.

Doesn't GIL make Python multithreading completely meaningless? Not really. Not all tasks require full, continuous power of a CPU, just as not all dishes require a cook's attention. For example, solving scientific models to predict weather will exhaust a CPU's capacity but sending an http request to a server is largely waiting. We can classify tasks into two categories: CPU bound tasks and input/output (I/O) bound tasks. Here *bound* means the task is limited by certain resources or bottlenecks.

1. CPU bound tasks are limited by the speed of CPUs. They are computationally heavy and make the CPUs busy. Examples include scientific computation, video compressing, bitcoin mining if you choose to mine with CPU.

2. I/O bound tasks are limited by the speed of input and output. They depend on external components or systems' performance. For example, reading and writing to the disk, sending and receiving files from the internet, etc. During the life cycle of an I/O bound task, a CPU is mostly idle.

If a Python process has multiple threads, the operating system will schedule each thread to have access to the CPU in a preemptive fashion. Being preemptive means the operating system by default *forces* the thread that currently runs to give up the CPU without asking whether it is a good time to do so. Such shifting between threads is so fast that they happen millions of times before you even notice.

If these threads are executing I/O bound tasks, it is totally fine! If they are human, they probably will say: hey CPU, I don't need you, I am waiting for my data from the disk.

Ultimately, the I/O bound tasks can wait together, therefore *progress* together.

Looking back at the cooking example, roast chicken and beef stew can be considered I/O bound dishes. Salad and poke bowls are *cook-bound* dishes. I have seen experienced cooks oversee the preparation of 40 Tofu stews in Koreatown in Los Angeles, but I never see any cook mixing seaweed in three bowls simultaneously.

If there is no real multithreading in Python, does it mean that with GIL, thread safety is guaranteed? Not really. It depends on at what level we are talking about thread safety. Yes, the threads will not compete for the shared resources at the same time, but it doesn't mean that they will mess the status up.

Here is an example, if two chefs are going to need the same bowl, one is going to make a rice pudding and another one is going to make kimchi. If right in the middle of the pudding making, the second chef just blindly obtains the *ownership* of the bowl and puts some kimchi into the bowl. When the first chef *resumes* the ownership of the bowl, I am pretty sure the chef will go crazy. A Python interpreter is thread safe, but it doesn't necessarily make a Python program thread safe if the logics overlay each other.

MULTIPROCESSING FOR CPU BOUND TASKS

In this section, we will dive into the Python concurrent pattern that is backed by *real* parallel computing: multiprocessing.

Before we start, I need to explain one more concept clarification and introduce probably one of the most powerful python code analysis tools I know.

First, multiprocessing may not happen on the Python-level, oftentimes you don't know that your Python code utilizes multiprocessing at C-level if you import a library that is written in C, C++ or Fortran. These are not considered multiprocessing in Python in this book. Similarly, multithreading in other languages evoked from Python are not considered multithreading in Python.

Second, let me introduce you to viztracer,[1] a Python logger, profiler and visualization tool. It supports multiprocessing and multithreading Python code and presents the result in an informative and pleasing way. Note that viztracer does have some impact on the speed of the code. If it skews the code performance, you can run your code without it to assess the impact.

It is very easy to install and use viztracer just follow code snippet 3.1. You can start visualizing your code traces in three lines. Suppose your *code* is in main.py and we use the default output file name *result.json*.

```
pip install viztracer

viztracer main.py

vizviewer result.json
```

CODE 3.1   Install and use viztracer to run *main.py* and visualize its result.

Now, we are ready to dive in. Let's first start with a basic example. We throw a million iterations of simple math computation to each process. And totally we have three such processes. The following code should be self-explanatory. Each process is given a different argument, starts and then *joins* on the main process, which simply means that the main process will wait on the spawned computing process to finish. Let's call this script *multiprocessing_basic.py* as shown in code snippet 3.2.

```
from multiprocessing import Process
import math

def f(x):
    for _ in range(1_000_000):
        x = math.sqrt(x) if x > 1.000001 else 2*x
    return x * x



if __name__ == '__main__':
    processes = [Process(target=f, args=(x,)) for x in [1.1, 2.1,
3.1]]
    for p in processes:
        p.start()
    for p in processes:
        p.join()
```

CODE 3.2   Basic multiprocessing example.

Use viztracer to profile this snippet. We have the following visualization. Note that based on your computer's computing power and number of physical cores, the actual time may vary, and the process identifiers will, for sure, be different.

From Figure 3.7, we can clearly see that there are four processes. We started the main process, and it spawns three more processes. Zoom into the main process and one of the spawned processes as shown in Figure 3.8. You can see there is only one thread in each of them. The graph shown on the right is called flame graph, but inverted opposed to the general usage. It decomposes the dependency relationships of the code and separates the running program in the time domain.

Next, we zoom into the minimal unit of our code, a `math.sqrt()` function call. As you can see in Figure 3.9, the selected call takes about 20 nanoseconds, which is quite fast. From the flame graph, you can also see this call comes from the code sample 3.2, line 7. Note that the call before it takes a longer time, so it is not always uniform. To achieve the same precision, the low-level implementation of *math.sqrt* may need to perform more iterations at the C-level. This is something that viztracer won't be able to log.

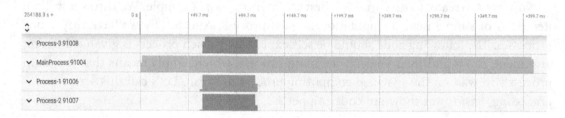

FIGURE 3.7 Four processes from `multiprocessing _ basic.py`.

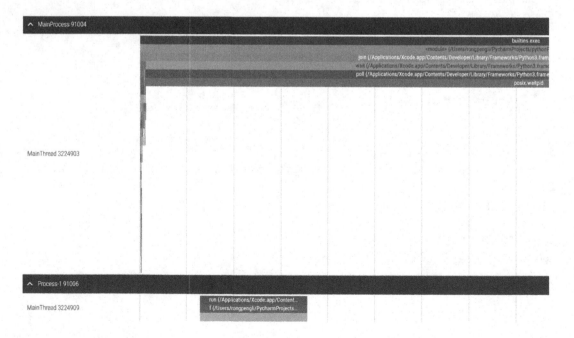

FIGURE 3.8 Each process has only one thread.

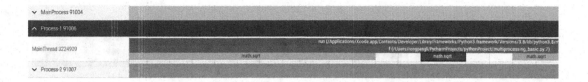

FIGURE 3.9   A *math.sqrt* call.

The management of processes and threads can be done systematically through a concept called *pool*. A pool is an object that you can submit tasks to without worrying about the creation and termination of process and threads. You can submit tasks using the *map* method and retrieve the results directly. Code snippet 3.3 is the pool version of code snippet 3.2. It is shorter and cleaner.

```python
from multiprocessing import Pool
import math

def f(x):
    for _ in range(1_000_000):
        x = math.sqrt(x) if x > 1.000001 else 2*x
    return x*x


if __name__ == '__main__':
    with Pool(3) as p:
        p.map(f, [1.1, 2.1, 3.1])
```

CODE 3.3   Use a process pool to run tasks.

However, if you viztrace it, the main process has three additional threads. They are introduced by using the pool pattern. Figure 3.10 looks strange, right? We know that GIL prevents multiple threads from running simultaneously but they look like they run at the same time.

This is due to a limitation of viztracer. If you are interested in diving deeper, Maarten Breddels has a great blog post[2] explaining the combination of Linux *perf* and viztracer to

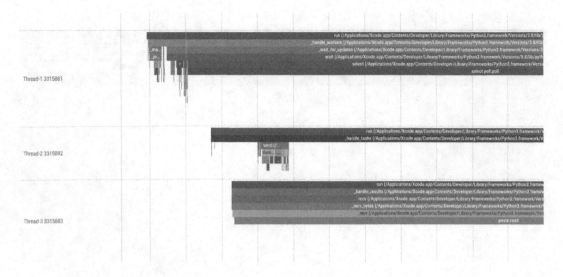

FIGURE 3.10   Three more threads are generated in main process.

solve this issue. I found that in other cases that if you explicitly create and manage threads, the issue is gone. We will see an example in the next section.

Parallel Pandas Apply in pandarallel

It's time to see multiprocessing in the real world. The star project pandarallel[3] is a library that enables parallel data manipulation of pandas DataFrame objects.

In Pandas, you can manipulate a column using the *apply()* method. The following code snippet 3.4 is a typical example that creates a bool variable that indicates the leap year status for DataFrame *df*.

```
def is_leap_year(year):
    if year % 400 == 0:
        return True
    elif year % 100 == 0:
        return False
    elif year % 4 == 0:
        return True
    else:
        return False


df["is_leap"] = df["year"].apply(is_leap_year)
```

CODE 3.4   A normal Pandas apply example.

However, this operation is done linearly. If the DataFrame is very large, it can take a long time. What pandarallel does is that for the apply method and similar operations, it shadows the default method that a DataFrame has inherently with a parallel, multiprocessing version.

Visually, the process contains three steps, which can be considered a *map-reduce* pattern as shown in Figure 3.11.

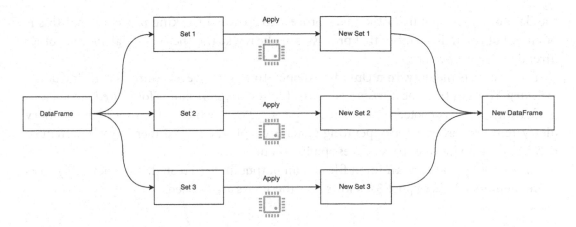

FIGURE 3.11   pandarallel multiprocessing.

1. Segment the dataset into smaller sizes.

2. Apply the data manipulation on each subset with multiprocessing.

3. Collect the results back and concatenate them together.

Let's examine each stage. You will find a practical program that utilizes multiprocessing will have to solve many subtle problems besides multiprocessing.

pandarallel implements a utility function called *chunk()*, and applies it to different data types in pandas like DataFrame, Series and other *group_by* objects. It simply returns a list of slices objects which can be used to *slice* an *Iterable* object. Let's take the most basic DataFrame, for example. Code snippet 3.5 is taken from data_types/dataframe.py[4] file.

```
@staticmethod
def get_chunks(
    nb_workers: int, data: pd.DataFrame, **kwargs
) -> Iterator[pd.DataFrame]:
    user_defined_function_kwargs =
kwargs["user_defined_function_kwargs"]

    axis_int = get_axis_int(user_defined_function_kwargs)
    opposite_axis_int = 1 - axis_int

    for chunk_ in chunk(data.shape[opposite_axis_int],
nb_workers):
        yield data.iloc[chunk_] if axis_int == 1 else data.iloc[:,
chunk_]
```

CODE 3.5   DataFrame slicing logic.

The *nb_workers* variable is the number of processes that will perform the data manipulation. By default, it is the number of physical cores of the machine. The question now is where the sliced subset will be stored, temporarily? Well, you can choose to not store the data but passing it from the main process to spawned working processes, but this is often not optimal. Remember that processes are heavy, so they better not talk to each other directly to stay efficient.

The answer is memory. In a Unix-based operating system, everything is a file including *memory*. You can treat the *dev/shm* path as a file system. *shm* stands for *shared memory*. In pandarallel, this is denoted with *MEMORY _ FS _ ROOT*, which is the root of the memory file system. However, not all operating systems enable the shared memory file system so pandarallel also has the cross-process piping mode.

For each physical core, an input file and an output file are created. This inevitably costs more memory. Code snippet 3.6 shows how these files are defined.

```
input_files = [
    NamedTemporaryFile(
        prefix=PREFIX_INPUT, suffix=SUFFIX, dir=MEMORY_FS_ROOT,
delete=False
    )
    for _ in range(nb_workers)
]

output_files = [
    NamedTemporaryFile(
        prefix=PREFIX_OUTPUT, suffix=SUFFIX, dir=MEMORY_FS_ROOT,
delete=False
    )
    for _ in range(nb_workers)
]
```

CODE 3.6   Each worker will have an input file and an output file.

There is a theory in computer science that computing power can be considered a currency. You can use computing power to buy other stuff like better user experiences. If you don't have enough computing power, you will have to sacrifice other assets. In this case, the *memory space*. The principle of no free lunch is applicable in this case.

Next, let's see the core of pandarallel as shown in code snippet 3.7.

```
pool = CONTEXT.Pool(nb_workers)
results_promise = pool.starmap_async(wrapped_work_function,
work_args_list)
pool.close()
```

CODE 3.7   Assign pandas tasks to workers.

Because Windows and Unix-based operating systems have different mechanisms of spawning new processes, *CONTEXT* is created based on the running operating system earlier. The process pool evokes the `starmap _ async` method to run the data transformation task in parallel.

Here are two takeaways of these two lines. First, the *starmap_async* method is essentially a *map* method as we have seen earlier, which can take multiple arguments as a zipped Iterable. The *star* essentially means the * character in **args* that unpacks the args Iterable.

Second, the mapping is done in an *async* way such that the returned value *results_promise* is not a list of processed datasets, but a *promise* object. A promise object can be treated literally as a promise that says, hey, I will grab the result for you in a later. Here is the promise that you can check often. The *result_promise* has a type of *AsyncResult* that belongs to the pool module. It has methods like *get()*, *ready()* and *successful()* that you can call to explicitly retrieve the results with a timeout, check whether it completes and whether it completes without error. We will discuss the asynchronous computing pattern in more detail in the next chapter.

Now, let's use viztracer to analyze the following code snippet 3.8 that utilizes pandarallel.

```python
import pandas as pd
import math
from pandarallel import pandarallel
import numpy as np

pandarallel.initialize(progress_bar=False)

df_size = int(1e4)
df = pd.DataFrame(dict(a=np.random.randint(
    1, 8, df_size), b=np.random.rand(df_size)))

def func(x):
    return math.sin(x.a**2) + math.sin(x.b**2)

res_parallel = df.parallel_apply(func, axis=1)
```

CODE 3.8   Run a heavy pandas job with pandarallel.

From the logging information as shown in snippet 3.9, I would expect 11 processes: one main process and ten worker processes.

```
INFO: Pandarallel will run on 10 workers.
INFO: Pandarallel will use standard multiprocessing data transfer
(pipe) to transfer data between the main process and workers.
Total Entries: 1052816
```

CODE 3.9   Logging information from the execution of snippet 3.8.

However, viztracer shows 12 processes in Figure 3.12. What is the *SyncManager* process?

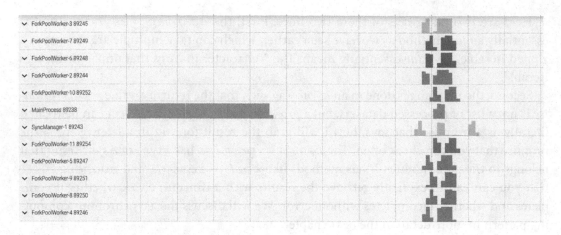

FIGURE 3.12   pandarallel has one more process called *SyncManager*.

The sync manager process is a process that maintains an object called manager and its associated objects, which are shared among other processes. In this case, it maintains a queue object that each worker process can put a tuple into, updating the process running status.

First, a queue object is created by a manager as highlighted in code snippet 3.10.

```
manager: SyncManager = CONTEXT.Manager()
master_workers_queue = manager.Queue()
```

CODE 3.10   Creation of the queue object.

The *master_worker_queue* is then passed to every worker process as part of the *work_args_list*. During the run, each worker can put messages into this queue in a first-in, first-out pattern, for example, whether the process runs successfully or not as illustrated in code snippet 3.11.

```
# code skipped
    with output_file_path.open("wb") as file_descriptor:
        pickle.dump(result, file_descriptor)

    master_workers_queue.put((worker_index, WorkerStatus.Success,
None))

except:
    master_workers_queue.put((worker_index, WorkerStatus.Error,
None))
    raise
```

CODE 3.11   Workers put data into the shared queue.

However, the main process reads from this queue (code snippet 3.12).

```
message: Tuple[int, WorkerStatus, Any] = master_workers_queue.
get()
worker_index, worker_status, payload = message
```

CODE 3.12   Master process reads from the shared queue.

You may wonder, why is this piece of information needed? The reason is that although each worker process runs rather independently, pandarallel maintains a progress bar chart that shows how much work has been done for each process. It needs information from all processes. On Jupyter notebook, it is like Figure 3.13.

You can enable the progress bar when initializing pandarallel. Each progress bar is updated by the logic in snippet 3.13:

```
# initialization of the progress bar
pandarallel.initialize(progress_bar = True)

# update of the progress bar

if worker_status == WorkerStatus.Success:
    progresses[worker_index] = progresses_length[worker_index]
    progress_bars.update(progresses)
elif worker_status == WorkerStatus.Running:
    progress = cast(int, payload)
    progresses[worker_index] = progress

    if next(generation) % nb_workers == 0:
        progress_bars.update(progresses)
elif worker_status == WorkerStatus.Error:
    progress_bars.set_error(worker_index)
    progress_bars.update(progresses)
```

CODE 3.13   Progress bar gets updated according to the information in the shared queue.

At this moment, we have decomposed the core of pandarallel into basic pieces: how the data are passed/shared, how processes are spawned and how the running statuses are reported to the main process.

DataFrame transformation is CPU bounded, how about I/O bound tasks?

FIGURE 3.13   Progress bar.

MULTITHREADING FOR I/O BOUND TASKS

Let's first confirm that multithreading is no worse or even better than multiprocessing for I/O bound tasks.

First, let's try a CPU bound task as a benchmark. Run code snippet 3.14 with viztracer.

```python
import time
from multiprocessing import Process
from threading import Thread
import math


def f(x):
    for _ in range(10_000_000):
        x = math.sqrt(x) if x > 1.000001 else 2*x
    return x * x


if __name__ == '__main__':
    start = time.time()
    processes = [Process(target=f, args=(x,)) for x in [1.1, 2.1,
3.1]]
    for p in processes:
        p.start()
    for p in processes:
        p.join()
    end = time.time()
    process_time = end - start

    start = time.time()
    threads = [Thread(target=f, args=(x,)) for x in [1.1, 2.1,
3.1]]
    for t in threads:
        t.start()
    for t in threads:
        t.join()
    end = time.time()
    thread_time = end - start

    print(f"Multiprocessing time: {process_time:.2f} seconds")
    print(f"Multithreading time: {thread_time:.2f} seconds")
```

CODE 3.14   Benchmark code for CPU bound tasks.

On my desktop, the multiprocessing version finishes in about 1.87 seconds and the multithreading version finishes in about 3.13 seconds.

At the process level shown in Figure 3.14, we have three spawned processes that do the computation. On the contrary, the highlighted part is where the multithreading computation *actually* happens.

Now, zoom into the main process. We see three threads are spawned, and it is very clear that no two threads can run at the same time in Figure 3.15. The GIL is real.

The longer the computation lasts, the less effect the overhead has, therefore multiprocessing is more suitable for multithreading.

How about I/O bound tasks? The most typical I/O bound task is probably an http request. The key change of the snippet above is to replace the mathematical function *f()* with *retrieve _ homepage()*. I am leaving the implementation to you. After you are done, run your code, which should look like snippet 3.15, with viztracer.

```
newspapers = ['https://www.nytimes.com/',
              'https://www.theguardian.com/',
              'https://www.huffingtonpost.com/',
              'https://www.bbc.com/']
```

```
def retrieve_homepage(newspaper):
    # Write a multiprocessing version and a multithreading version
of this function
    response = requests.get(newspaper)
```

CODE 3.15

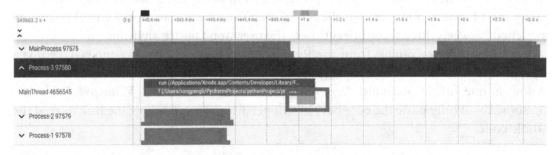

FIGURE 3.14 Multiprocessing vs multithreading on CPU bound tasks.

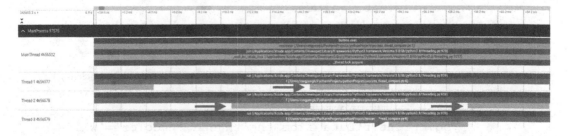

FIGURE 3.15 No two threads can run at the same time.

On my desktop, the multiprocessing version takes about 1.29 seconds, and the multithreading version takes about 0.76 seconds. Running multiple times, the multithreading version is always faster than the multiprocessing version. If you check the flame graph, you will see that most of the time, the spawned threads are just doing connecting, handshaking, etc. The CPU can handle multiple of them at the same time.

As described in earlier section, the CPU very quickly shifts between threads to make progress on each one. This is called preemptive as we have no explicit control over when the CPU should make the shift, and the CPU asks no opinions from the threads. You may wonder what's the point of having multithreading in Python.

Let's check one specific use case of multithreading: graphical user interface (GUI). Even without real parallel multithreading, Python multithreading can also become handy. Video games are probably a better example for multithreading programming in C++ as performance is the key, but we are talking about Python now.

Imagine the most typical use case of interacting with a GUI application. Oftentimes, there are many different components that constitute the application: the visuals, the sound, the interactions, etc.

Suppose you are using an RSS reader to browse news. RSS reader fetches the headlines for you to glance at. If you click one headline, the reader then fetches the whole content of the article. If the RSS reader is single-threaded, the application won't respond to your scrolling or clicking gestures. You will have to wait for the content to load, then the reader becomes responsive again. This is a horrible user experience.

There should be one thread dedicated to content fetching and another thread dedicated to responding to user gestures for optimal experiences. You may wonder if the application is written in Python, won't GIL prevent it from doing so? Remember, a CPU is way faster than humans. Between two clicks and even two screen frames, the CPU has already switched between threads countless times. The user won't notice anything.

Let's look at one example from the Python open source library PySimpleGUI.[5] It is a Python library for building simple graphical user interfaces with more than 10K stars. Below is one official example: *Demo_Multithreaded_Write_Event_Value.py*.[6] For space reasons, I will only paste the core part in snippet 3.16. You can follow the link to read the whole code.

```
while True:
        event, values = window.read()
        sg.cprint(event, values)
        if event == sg.WIN_CLOSED or event == 'Exit':
            break
        if event.startswith('Start'):
            threading.Thread(target=the_thread, args=(window,),
daemon=True).start()
        if event == THREAD_EVENT:
            sg.cprint(f'Data from the thread ', colors='white on
purple', end='')
```

```
        sg.cprint(f'{values[THREAD_EVENT]}', colors='white on
red')
    window.close()
```

CODE 3.16   Certain events are handled with new threads.

The window object listens to events, which are essentially user interactions with the application. For example, closing the window is an event and clicking a button is also an event. In the second if statement, if the event starts with 'Start', a new thread is created to run the *the _ thread* function. You will see by clicking a button called *Start A Thread* will trigger such an event (code snippet 3.17). What does *the _ thread* do?

```
def the_thread(window):
    \"""
    The thread that communicates with the application through the
window's events.
    Once a second wakes and sends a new event and associated value
to the window
    \"""
    i = 0
    while True:
        time.sleep(1)
        window.write_event_value(
            '-THREAD-', (threading.current_thread().name, i))
        i += 1
```

CODE 3.17   *the _ thread* periodically writes to the active window.

It is merely a function that sleeps for a while and then sends some info back for the window to render on the GUI. It is not CPU intensive as *time.sleep()* puts CPU to idle.

Now, let's run the program with viztracer. Note that your Python version must have the latest tkinter installed. The Python version I am using on my MacOS is 3.10 for this part of the demo. You can install it using Homebrew as shown in snippet 3.18.

```
brew install python-tk@3.10
```

CODE 3.18   Install Python with tkinter.

Run the demo, a new window should pop up as Figure 3.16.

Now, randomly click the *Start A Thread* button three times. Periodic messages will appear in the active window as shown in Figure 3.17. Close the window, in the viztracer's visualization, we will see three threads periodically send information to the window as shown in Figure 3.18. That's exactly what *the _ thread* is supposed to do.

There is one process which contains one main thread and three spawned worker threads.

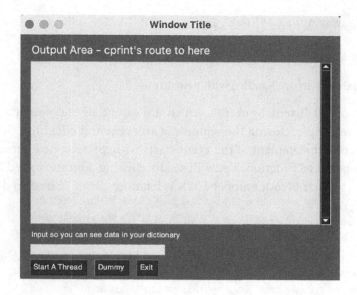

FIGURE 3.16 Demo GUI.

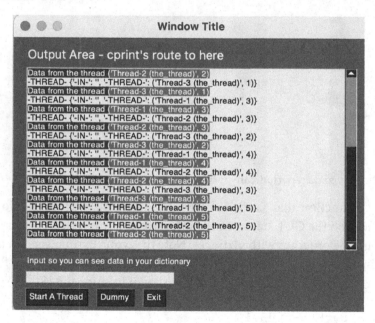

FIGURE 3.17 Three working threads write to the UI.

We do see in Figure 3.18 that these three threads sleep for most of the time. The example may be simple, but the idea is clear: if you are fast enough, people won't notice that you are multithreading. It is like in the remote working age, some people choose to work for more than two companies secretly: if you are productive enough and some tasks are basically boring and only require periodic checks, nobody will notice.

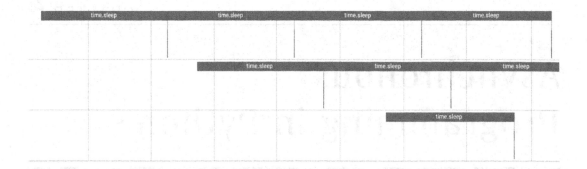

FIGURE 3.18   Worker threads that sleep periodically.

SUMMARY

In this long chapter, we started from basic concepts and investigated the discrepancies between general programming language and Python: the GIL's role. We then jump on the multiprocessing examples from pandarallel and multithreading examples from PySimpleGUI. We understand their use cases.

Does concurrent programming always require multiprocessing or multithread? What if we want to control when and where should a thread yield CPU ownership? We will find out in the next chapter.

NOTES

1 https://github.com/gaogaotiantian/viztracer
2 https://www.maartenbreddels.com/perf/jupyter/python/tracing/gil/2021/01/14/Tracing-the-Python-GIL.html
3 https://github.com/nalepae/pandarallel
4 https://github.com/nalepae/pandarallel/blob/master/pandarallel/data_types/dataframe.py
5 https://github.com/PySimpleGUI/PySimpleGUI
6 https://github.com/PySimpleGUI/PySimpleGUI/blob/master/DemoPrograms/Demo_Multithreaded_Write_Event_Value.py

## CHAPTER 4

Asynchronous Programming in Python

A SHIFT OF PARADIGM

In Chapter 3, we introduced concurrency as a *behavior* property. If a user interacts with an application and feels that the system is concurrent, then the user probably won't care about its implementation. At the implementation level, we studied how it is possible to achieve concurrency by utilizing *real* parallelism, multiprocessing, and *not-so-real* parallelism, multithreading limited by GIL. The former is suitable for CPU-bound tasks, and the latter is suitable for I/O-bound tasks.

For both cases, we are thinking from the perspective of time dimension, namely we care about how multiple tasks are carried out or whether they are carried out at a specific point in time. This perspective is particularly true for multithreading as we know the CPU jumps preemptively between threads and no threads are running at the exact same time.

Well, for I/O bound tasks, how about thinking from the perspective of I/O events? Let's study a real-world example.

Suppose you are organizing a chess game for charity. You invited 1 grandmaster to play against 5 hobbyists at the same time. The grandmaster is way better than the hobbyists, so he doesn't even need to think about each move. How should this 1-versus-5 game be organized?

The natural way is to play synchronously. The grandmaster waits for player 1 to make 1 move, then he makes his move and goes to play with player 2. At that time, player 2 may already make a move or may not. The grandmaster probably needs to wait.

What's worse is that players 3, 4 and 5 may be waiting too. Essentially, they are *blocked* by other players' thinking time.

If we want to simulate this game, what's more important is that we don't want to do multithreading as the CPU jumps between threads crazily fast. It is equivalent to the hobbyists grabbing the grandmaster's attention while the hobbyist is still thinking! The grandmaster will probably go nuts and quit.

DOI: 10.1201/9781003316909-5

This is where a new thinking paradigm needs to be introduced. We need to think from an event-driven perspective. In our 1-vs-5 game, the important events are player-x making a move. If nobody makes a move and just thinks, the grandmaster doesn't need to do anything. The grandmaster is so powerful that the games never get blocked by him.

In other words, a single thread *should* be enough to simulate the games as long as each game can give up the grandmaster's attention *willingly* and *cooperatively* and go back to *thinking* mode.

This is the shift of paradigm: from preemptive to co-operative, from time-driven to event-driven.

EVENT-DRIVEN SIMULATION

We need to solve two issues.

1. Each game needs to give up its *execution* willingly.

2. One player's thinking shouldn't block other players' games.

The first issue can be solved by using a generator function. A generator function has a *yield* keyword instead of a *return* keyword. The generator function *pauses* at the yield keyword and can be resumed by calling the *next()* function with the generator. Code snippet 4.1 is a classic example of a Fibonacci number generator.

```
def fibonacci():
    a, b = 0, 1
    while True:
        yield a
        a, b = b, a + b

fib = fibonacci()
for i in range(10):
    print(next(fib))
```

CODE 4.1   Classic Fibonacci function.

The *fib* object is a generator object. Every time we call the *next()* function, it runs 1 round of the infinite loop and yields one value of *a*. A generator doesn't *have to* yield anything. If it doesn't, it simply yields the privilege to run until the next *next()* is called. However, a generator can also accept an input by calling its *send()* method. Such a variant of function that can be non-preemptively suspended and resumed is often referred to as a coroutine.

Now, let's write a version of the chess game simulation in which each player lets the grandmaster go when the player starts thinking. It is code snippet 4.2.

```
import time
import random
```

```
from itertools import cycle

def play_chess(player_name):
    while True:
        # Generator function that simulates a player thinking for
a random amount of time between 1 to 10 seconds
        print(f"{player_name} is thinking...")
        yield
        time.sleep(random.uniform(1, 2))
        print(f"{player_name} made a move!")


def main():
    # The main function that simulates the chess game
    players = ['Player 1', 'Player 2', 'Player 3', 'Player 4',
'Player 5']
    player_gen = cycle((play_chess(player) for player in players))
    for player_g in player_gen:
        next(player_g)
if __name__ == "__main__":
    main()
```

CODE 4.2   Use a generator to yield the attention of the grand master.

Here, we see another way to create a generator: just replace the bracket of list comprehension with parentheses. (play _ chess(player) for player in players) creates a finite generator of length 5, we then use the *cycle* function to iterate it over and over again. Run it, and we see snippet 4.3 in the terminal.

```
Player 1 is thinking...
Player 2 is thinking...
Player 3 is thinking...
Player 4 is thinking...
Player 5 is thinking...
Player 1 made a move!
Player 1 is thinking...
Player 2 made a move!
Player 2 is thinking..
```

CODE 4.3   Output from code snippet 4.2.

This solves issue one that each game does give up the grandmaster's attention willingly. However, one player's thinking still blocks other players' actions. What we really want is that the order of different players' logging information will be mixed, and the grandmaster literally runs from table to table when a player raises hands and says: Hi, I just made a move.

We have two solutions.

Solution in code snippet 4.4 is to use the powerful asyncio library to turn the blocking *time.sleep()* into a non-blocking *asyncio.sleep()* and use the *async-await* pair to replace the generator's yield syntax.

```python
import asyncio
import random

async def play_chess(player_name):
    while True:
        await asyncio.sleep(random.uniform(1, 2))
        print(f"{player_name}'s made a move!")

async def main():
    players = ['Player 1', 'Player 2', 'Player 3', 'Player 4',
'Player 5']
    tasks = [play_chess(player) for player in players]
    await asyncio.gather(*tasks)
if __name__ == "__main__":
    asyncio.run(main())
```

CODE 4.4   Use `asyncio.sleep()` to unblock the player's thinking.

Okay, a lot of new syntax but don't worry.

By putting an *async* keyword in front of a function, we turn a regular Python function into a coroutine which means the coroutine can be suspended as resumed willingly.

The question is where: at where the *await* keyword is used. We call the objects that follow the *await* keywords *awaitable*. As the name suggests, they can be waited for. There are two most common awaitables.

1. Coroutine objects are awaitable as we already saw.

2. Future objects are also awaitable.

So, what's a future? A future instance represents a promise that should eventually be honored. In other words, you can hold on to the future instance and expect it to have a *final state* in a later time. For example, you order something at a food truck, and you get a number. This number is a future that indicates that your order will be fulfilled. A future can also be *canceled* just like you can cancel your food order.

We will talk more about the future in a later section.

In the *play_chess* coroutine, the code will pause when it goes to sleep and hand over the control back to the event loop. An event loop is a construct in programming that constantly waits for and dispatches events or messages. In our chess game example, there is no real-world event loop analogy. However, there is one in our restaurant/kitchen example in the last chapter: a waiter.

Suppose there is only one waiter in the restaurant, he greets people when *people enter the restaurant*, takes orders when *people sit down*, picks up the food when the chef *rings the bell.* He is always *watching and listening to* all kinds of events going on in the restaurants and acts responsively to each event.

A waiter is the center of the message in a restaurant. He is also a *scheduler* that decides which goes first, which goes later. If you ever went to a restaurant right after the pandemic was over when every restaurant was short staffed, you know what I am saying.

In pseudocode snippet 4.5, an event loop does the following.

```
initialize()
while event != quit
    event := receive_event()
    process_event(event)
```

CODE 4.5   Basic event loop as pseudocode.

In the asyncio version of the code, you can call `asyncio.get_event_loop()` to obtain the current running event loop. Before Python 3.7 when *async.run()* isn't available, the syntax to run a coroutine *coro()* is to access the event loop directly as shown in snippet 4.6.

```
loop = asyncio.get_event_loop()
loop.run_until_complete(coro())
```

CODE 4.6   Use the event loop object to schedule and run a coroutine.

Note that there are other implementations of event loop besides the default one that comes with asyncio. For example, uvloop[1] is another implementation of event loop which is advertised as 2–4 times faster than the built-in implementation.

Now, run the asyncio version code. We do see that the order of players making moves is randomized as shown in log snippet 4.7. It also runs much faster than the blocking version.

```
Player 3's made a move!
Player 4's made a move!
Player 2's made a move!
Player 5's made a move!
Player 1's made a move!
Player 3's made a move!
Player 2's made a move!
Player 5's made a move!
Player 4's made a move!
```

CODE 4.7   Player moves are randomized.

Next, let's use viztracer to analyze this piece of code and find out how many threads are being used. Just change the infinite while loop to a limited for loop, we get Figure 4.1, which shows that there is only one thread doing all the heavy lifting.

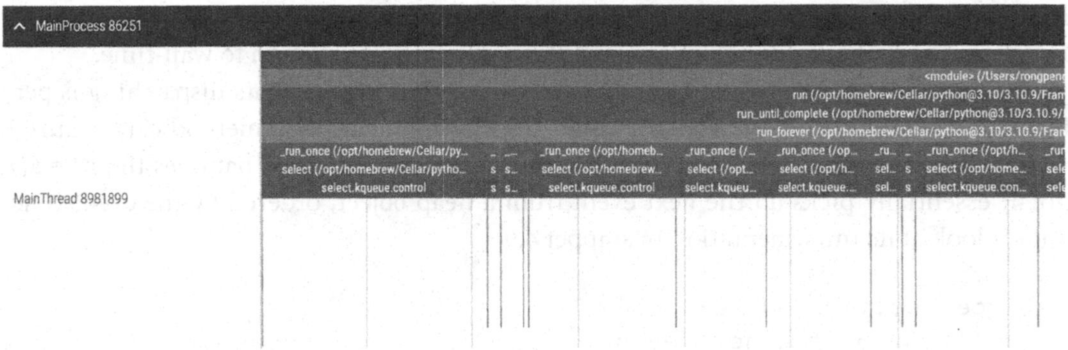

FIGURE 4.1   Five-player chess game simulation.

Another solution is to keep using the generator function as a coroutine. However, we must handle the scheduling ourselves. If you really want to implement your own event loop as an exercise, I encourage you to follow David Beazley's Build Your Own Async[2] workshop. It is the best on this topic. In this book, we are just going to investigate mature simulation libraries like *SimPy*[3] to handle all the scheduling, etc.

SimPy is a discrete-event simulation framework based on standard Python according to its GitHub readme. It defines a concept called *process*, essentially a coroutine, using generator functions that can run in an *environment*. The environment keeps track of which process goes faster and which goes later, etc. Code snippet 4.8 is the equivalent simulation written using *SimPy*. Note that *SymPy* is a different library we used in Chapter 2. It is about symbolic computing.

```python
import random
import simpy
import time

def play_chess(env, player_name):
    while True:
        yield env.timeout(random.uniform(1, 2))
        print(f"{env.now:.2f}: {player_name} made a move!")

def main():
    # The main simulation environment that simulates the chess
game
    env = simpy.rt.RealtimeEnvironment(factor=1)
    players = ['Player 1', 'Player 2', 'Player 3', 'Player 4',
'Player 5']
    for player in players:
        env.process(play_chess(env, player))
    env.run(until=float("inf"))
```

CODE 4.8   Use SymPy to simulate the chess games.

By default, SymPy will try to run the simulation in a virtual time as fast as possible. However, using the *RealtimeEnvironment* slows down the simulation to wall-time.

The SymPy library gives us a good taste how asynchronous events dispatching is performed. If you dive into the core.py[4] code, The environment has a method called *run()* which calls the *step()* method until the end of the simulation. What does the *step()* do? It essentially picks up the next event from a heap object, ordered by the event time. Take a look at its implementation in snippet 4.9.

```python
def step(self) -> None:
    """Process the next event.
    """
    try:
        self._now, _, _, event = heappop(self._queue)
    except IndexError:
        raise EmptySchedule()
    # skipped
```

CODE 4.9 *Step()* function pops an event out of the heap.

Well, how does the event loop, essentially the environment, know when and what the next event is? The Environment class has a *schedule* method that does exactly this as shown in snippet 4.10. It pushes an event that will happen in the future to the heap. Without specification, all events have a *NORMAL* priority.

```python
def schedule(
    self,
    event: Event,
    priority: EventPriority = NORMAL,
    delay: SimTime = 0,
) -> None:
    """Schedule an *event* with a given *priority* and a
*delay1."""
    heappush(self._queue,
                (self._now + delay, priority, next(self._eid),
event))
    # skip
```

CODE 4.10 *schedule()* function pushes an event to the heap.

The heap data structure has a unique property that the first item *self._queue[0]* is always the smallest one. In this case, the earliest event. By maintaining this heap structure, our environment always knows what the next event to simulate is.

When an event instance is initialized, an environment instance is passed to it. Therefore, an event can schedule itself by calling the environment instance's *schedule* method. There are plenty of examples in the events.py[5] source code which manage statuses and lifecycle of an event. This is a design pattern called dependency injection[6]: it simply means that you pass an instance of object A to object B to use instead of asking object B to construct itself.

SymPy runs like a loop and keeps fetching the next event to schedule it. Note that we humans naturally do this every day. When my wife asks me to buy some toilet paper when there is only one roll left, I basically schedule these two events in my mind and associate them together. Hopefully, I remember them next time I go shopping.

Alright. If asynchronous programming is so good, why not change all codes into asynchronous?

ASYNC AS A PATTERN

When writing this book, I was going to explain how an asynchronous wrapper works with an open source library called aiosqlite.[7] However, I realize that it is impossible to cover its source code without introducing quite some functional programming that belongs to the next chapter.

This is the typical case of leveling up yourself with advanced Python knowledge. Different concepts are convoluted so you must decouple them surgically. Our next chapter will cover function-related concepts with examples from aiosqlite and, from there, understand how these concepts make the synchronous-to-asynchronous wrapping possible.

So, what do we do in this section? In this section, I plan to clarify some myths. Earlier, I showed that the asynchronous codes are all running with one thread. This is to emphasize that asynchronous programming *can* achieve concurrency with only one thread. However, it doesn't mean that asynchronous code can *only* utilize one thread. In fact, the most fundamental difference between async code and plain multithreading code is that the programmer, rather than the operating system, takes over the wheel and decides when a task gives up the CPU. If multiple threads or even multiple processes are needed, so be it.

Let's walk through some examples.

First, let's wrap an io-blocking function with `async` and create a task with `asyncio` as shown in code snippet 4.11.

```python
import asyncio
import time

async def factorial(name, number):
    f = 1
    for i in range(2, number + 1):
        print(f"Task {name}: Compute factorial({number}),
currently i={i}...")
        time.sleep(1)
        f *= i
    print(f"Task {name}: factorial({number}) = {f}")

async def main():
    start = time.time()
    task_a = asyncio.create_task(factorial("A", 4))
```

```
    task_b = asyncio.create_task(factorial("B", 4))
    task_c = asyncio.create_task(factorial("C", 4))
    await asyncio.gather(task_a, task_b, task_c)
    end = time.time()
    total_time = end - start
    print(f"Total time: {total_time:.2f} seconds")
if __name__ == "__main__":
    asyncio.run(main())
```

CODE 4.11   Use `asyncio` to run io-blocking tasks.

factorial() is not a real coroutine because it doesn't specify a place where it gives up the CPU voluntarily. *create _ task* takes the *fake* coroutine and schedules them to run.

Unfortunately, the code runs slowly and completes in 9 seconds. viztracer tells us that there is only one thread, and it doesn't treat a thread-blocking io operation as asynchronous just because you run it with asyncio. It is clear in Figure 4.2.

Wait a minute, didn't the chess player example show that the players can think, aka *sleep()*, at the same time? No. These are two sleeps. *time.sleep()* will block the execution entirely if there is only one thread while *asyncio.sleep()* will only tell the event loop to look for other tasks to do so the coroutine can take a nap on its own.

However, asyncio can also create a task on another thread. The code is largely unchanged, with the following changes in snippet 4.12. Instead of using *create _ task()*, we use *to _ thread()*.

```
task_a = asyncio.to_thread(factorial)
task_b = asyncio.to_thread(factorial)
task_c = asyncio.to_thread(factorial)
```

CODE 4.12   Create tasks on a different thread.

> Note that if we want to pass different parameters to the *factorial* function, we must use the *functools.partial()*, which belongs to the next chapter.

FIGURE 4.2   Single thread doesn't work for io-blocking tasks.

FIGURE 4.3 *to_thread()* enables parallel *time.sleep()*.

Also, we need to remove the *async* in front of the definition of *factorial* because *to_thread()* only accepts a function. However, the return is a coroutine that can be awaited.

Let's check Figure 4.3 from viztracer. The snippet finishes in 3 seconds. This agrees with our conclusion from the previous chapter that multithreading is suitable for I/O bound tasks.

By the same token, we can also create a process and handle the return asynchronously. Is there something like the *pool* object we introduced in the last chapter that simplifies the workflow? The answer is yes. However, they belong to the *concurrent* module, not asyncio. And they return *futures*.

Recall that futures are also awaitable. Let's use the *concurrent.future* module to run the I/O bound tasks as shown in snippet 4.13.

```python
async def main():
    start = time.time()
    futures = [None, None, None]
    with concurrent.futures.ThreadPoolExecutor() as pool:
        for i in range(3):
            futures[i] = pool.submit(factorial)
        while True:
            if all([future.done() for future in futures]):
                break
            else:
                print("Checking future status at {}".format(time.
time() - start))
                time.sleep(0.5)
    end = time.time()
```

```
    total_time = end - start
    print(f"Total time: {total_time:.2f} seconds")
```

CODE 4.13 Use `concurrent.future` to run tasks in a thread pool.

We create a list of futures called *futures*. When we submit the jobs to the executor, we get a future back, whose status we can check. Then in the main thread, we periodically check its status every 0.5 second. When all futures are *done*, we stop checking.

Note that a significant difference between a coroutine and a future, who are both awaitables, is that a future will be executed whatsoever, but a coroutine will only run if we *await* for it. In the code above, we simply submitted the jobs to the pool without using the *await* keyword. A coroutine, however, must follow the *await* keyword.

This is a very typical case in real life too: an impatient customer keeps asking when his food is ready.

Let's check the viztracer flame graph Figure 4.4.

Imagine that we have both I/O-bound tasks and CPU-bound tasks, we can submit the I/O-bound tasks to the thread executor pool and the CPU-bound tasks to the process executor pool. The advantage is that you can have a unified way to handle those futures.

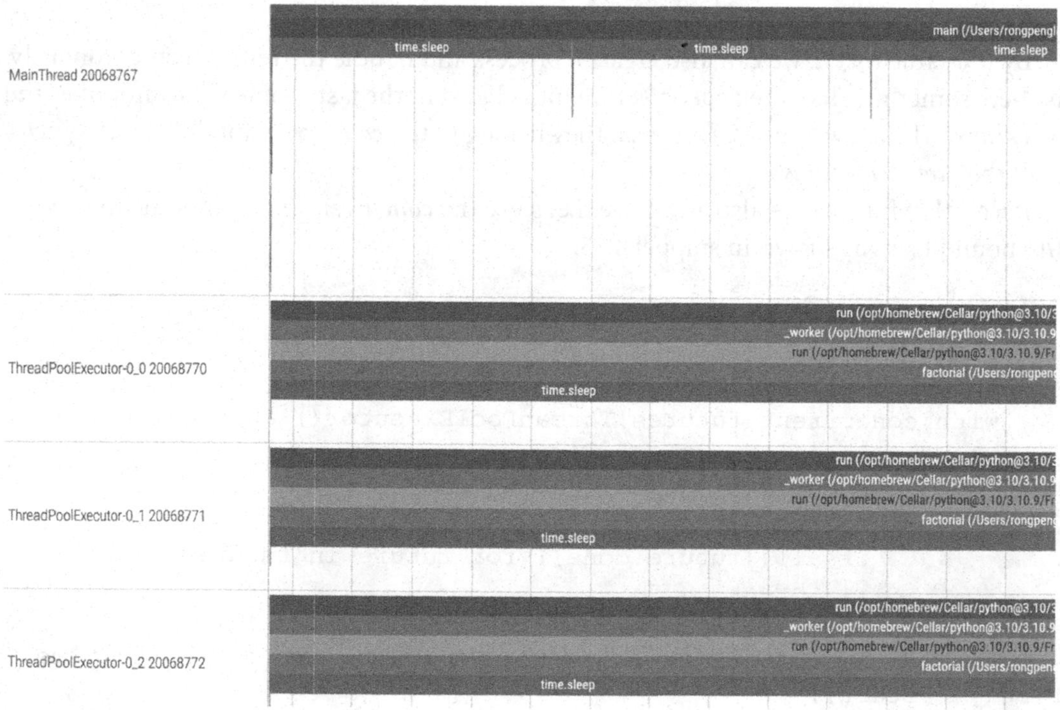

FIGURE 4.4 Frequent checks on the main thread.

SUMMARY

In this chapter, we covered the pattern shifting from thinking in the time dimension to thinking in the event dimension. We used a chess game as an example to demonstrate the paradigm shift. Then we peeked into an event-driven simulation library to understand how the scheduling works. Asyncio creates an event loop to schedule the coroutines. We also emphasized that asynchronous doesn't necessarily work on only one thread, but merely a pattern.

Although we covered examples how you can submit normal tasks to *concurrent.futures* executors so they return awaitable futures. However, we deliberately skipped the example of turning some synchronous operations natively asynchronous. Let's cover this big project in our next chapter.

APPENDIX

For developers who know how code runs at a lower level, I think it is time to shed some light on how single-thread asynchronous programming is implemented at a lower level. In procedural programming, each thread maintains one call *stack*: an ordered pile of frames. For simplicity, we can think of frames as cards that contain instructions or data. Each time the CPU picks up one card and does exactly what the card tells it to do. When a program starts, the stack is initialized as an empty list, the instructions are pushed into the stack in a last in, first out (LIFO) pattern. If you call a function `first_function()` which calls another `second_function()` in the code, the `second_function()` will be on top of the `first_function()` and therefore gets executed first so it can handle some results to the `first_function()`. This abstraction is called the stack machine.

Figure 4.5 is a simplification of how the stack machine works. The CPU uses an instruction pointer to track what the program is executing. When a new function is called, it is

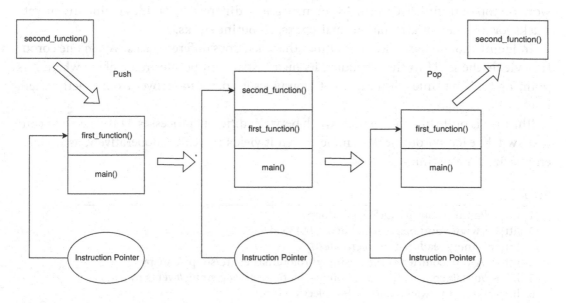

FIGURE 4.5   Stack machine.

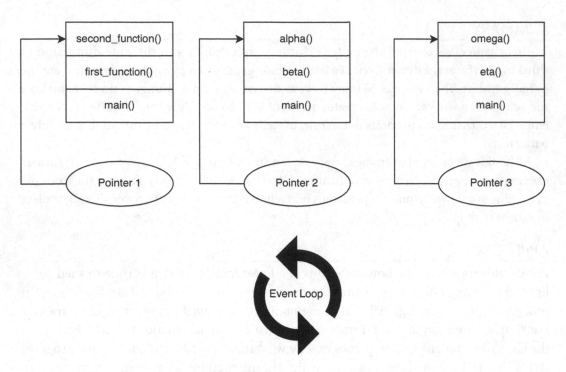

FIGURE 4.6   Multiple stack scenario.

pushed to the top of the stack. After it finishes, it pops out of the stack. This process continues until the *main* function returns.

In a one-stack scenario, it is impossible to jump executions between different tasks as the instruction pointer is only tracking at the top of the stack. We can't pile unfinished work on top of unfinished work. As you may guess, different coroutines maintain separate stacks, or to differentiate from normal stacks, coroutine stacks.

In Figure 4.6, we have three coroutines that each does different tasks. When one coroutine yields the CPU to the scheduler, its *own* instruction pointer remembers where it is pointing to. Next time when the event loop picks it up, it can recover from exactly where it left.

The idea is quite like the context switch between different processes. Different from context switch, each coroutine determines when it yields the CPU cooperatively, as we have emphasized many times.

NOTES

1 https://github.com/MagicStack/uvloop
2 https://www.youtube.com/watch?v=Y4Gt3Xjd7G8
3 https://simpy.readthedocs.io/en/latest/
4 https://gitlab.com/team-simpy/simpy/-/blob/master/src/simpy/core.py
5 https://gitlab.com/team-simpy/simpy/-/blob/master/src/simpy/events.py
6 https://martinfowler.com/articles/injection.html
7 https://github.com/omnilib/aiosqlite

## CHAPTER 5

Power Up Your Python Functions

INTRODUCTION

This chapter's title is Power Up Your Python Functions. This is not a chapter about pure functional programming, and Python is not a pure functional programming language. However, Python assimilated a lot of great stuff from functional programming in its development. When writing Python codes, it is possible to combine the best from different paradigms like object-oriented programming, procedural programming and functional programming. Don't be a fundamentalist, be Pythonic.

Let's find out how to 10X Python functions.

THE DECORATOR FOR RETRYING A FUNCTION

Suppose we are writing an application that talks to an external service. Your application talks to more than 20 API endpoints managed by the service. However, the external service is known to have several issues. Some API endpoints are unstable that 40% of the time the request will fail even if you did nothing wrong. The API endpoints are also rate limited so that you can't exceed a request frequency like once every second.

In general, you want to retry the requests in a controlled fashion. The plain Python implementation will look like code snippet 5.1.

```python
import time
from random import random
TIME_DELTA = 1
IS_SUCCESS = False


def post_to_endpoint():
    return random() < 0.6
```

DOI: 10.1201/9781003316909-6

```
if __name__ == '__main__':
    while not IS_SUCCESS:
        IS_SUCCESS = post_to_endpoint()
        time.sleep(TIME_DELTA)
```

CODE 5.1   Plain implementation of function retrying.

This code works, but if different endpoints have different failure rate or rate limits, we will have to write the loop logic everywhere, which creates a huge amount of code duplication.

How do we elegantly prepare functions like *post _ to _ endpoint()* to run against the nasty services?

The answer is to use a decorator. A decorator is a function (for most cases, sometimes a decorator can be implemented as a class with a __ call __ dunder method) that takes a function in and outputs another function. A decorator extends the functionality of the input function.

In Python, functions are first-class citizens. You can create a list of functions, pass a function to another function as input and return a function from a function. For example, the pattern in snippet 5.2 is natural in Python.

```
def prepare_function(fn):
    # do something about fn so it automatically retries
    return fn

prepared_post_to_endpoint = prepare_function(post_to_endpoint)
```

CODE 5.2   Pass a function to another function.

A decorator is a syntax sugar for such a pattern. It magically hides the details behind the scenes and eliminates the code duplication. Code snippet 5.3 is my simplistic, ugly implementation of the *prepare_function()*.

```
@prepare_function
def post_to_endpoint():
    return random() < 0.6


def prepare_function(fn, time_delta=1):
    # do something about fn so it automatically retries
    def new_fun():
        is_success = False
        while not is_success:
            is_success = fn()
            time.sleep(time_delta)
    return new_fun
```

CODE 5.3   A naïve implementation of *prepare _ function()* decorator.

As this function retry scenario is so common, there is already a popular one-file *retrying*[1] library written in Python. It supports several popular usage scenarios. I am just quoting its readme now.

Snippet 5.4 shows two examples: retry only for a certain period or retry with a fixed inter-try time interval.

```
@retry(stop_max_delay=10000)
def stop_after_10_s():
    print "Stopping after 10 seconds"

@retry(wait_fixed=2000)
def wait_2_s():
    print "Wait 2 second between retries"
```

CODE 5.4   Retrying for different cases.

Before diving into its implementation, let's brainstorm how such a decorator should be implemented if you are assigned the task.

Retrying is a *stateful* process, something must be responsible for keeping track of whether the retry is successful, how many retry opportunities are left, etc. It is best to implement a class to bookkeep those configurations and manage the retry behavior. Such a class should be able to store and call the underlined function.

> In computing, *stateful* refers to systems that maintain a record of previous interactions, while *stateless* systems do not. Stateful systems are more complex while stateless systems are simpler.

As we anticipated, the retrying library implements a `Retrying` class that takes a lot of arguments to initialize as shown in code snippet 5.5.

```
class Retrying(object):

    def __init__(self,
                stop=None, wait=None,
                stop_max_attempt_number=None,
                stop_max_delay=None,
                wait_fixed=None,):
        # skip
        pass
```

CODE 5.5   `Retrying` class takes many arguments to initialize.

The real decorator `retry()` is simply a function to pass the arguments to the `Retrying` class by creating two wrapper functions based on whether the retrying logic is simple or complicated. Check out code snippet 5.6.

```python
def retry(*dargs, **dkw):
    """
    Decorator function that instantiates the Retrying object
    @param *dargs: positional arguments passed to Retrying object
    @param **dkw: keyword arguments passed to the Retrying object
    """
    # support both @retry and @retry() as valid syntax
    if len(dargs) == 1 and callable(dargs[0]):
        def wrap_simple(f):

            @six.wraps(f)
            def wrapped_f(*args, **kw):
                return Retrying().call(f, *args, **kw)

            return wrapped_f

        return wrap_simple(dargs[0])

    else:
        def wrap(f):

            @six.wraps(f)
            def wrapped_f(*args, **kw):
                return Retrying(*dargs, **dkw).call(f, *args, **kw)

            return wrapped_f

        return wrap
```

CODE 5.6 The *Retrying* class is wrapped inside the retry function.

Here, the *dargs* and *dkw* variables stand for decorator arguments and decorator keyword arguments. They are the configurations. As we brainstormed and shown in code snippet 5.7, the Retrying class has a call method that invokes the function fn, whose core logic is still a while loop.

```python
def call(self, fn, *args, **kwargs):
    start_time = int(round(time.time() * 1000))
    attempt_number = 1
    while True:
        if self._before_attempts:
            self._before_attempts(attempt_number)
        # skip
```

CODE 5.7 The call method keeps retrying the argument function.

I will leave the rest of the reading for yourself as it is quite straightforward. The moral of the story is that you can build a colossus behind a decorator and the user won't know its existence. The user won't know that a Retrying instance is created to manage the retrying states and possible exceptions. The user only cares about whether a function is enhanced to do the desired task.

Does this sound familiar? It is in fact very similar to metaclass. When developers create the *retry()* function decorator, they don't know what function it is going to decorate but they know the function may have to run several times to succeed. Similarly, a metaclass doesn't know what class will be defined but it controls the behavior of the classes.

In fact, we also have class decorators which enhance classes: it takes a class as input and returns another class as output. It is not as powerful as metaclass but often easier to understand and maintain.

Next, let's look at a special kind of decorator: context managers.

CONTEXT MANAGER IN A NUTSHELL

Oftentimes, a function is not standalone. A function's successful run may require certain resources like established database connections, opened file descriptor, etc. After a function run, some resources tearing down may be required like releasing a thread lock, notifying other services: I am done.

There are real-world examples as well. Here is a naive one: suppose you are a sports coach. Each time before the athletes go to the field, you want to make sure they are in good shape by warming them up. Each time they finish exercising or competing, you want to make sure they get enough stretch and relaxation. No matter what sports they do, they have to follow these steps. The warmup always precedes the sports, and the stretching always follows the sports immediately.

In other words, in the context of sports, some activities need to be managed in an orderly fashion.

How do we enforce such an order structure? We need a context manager. The simplest context manager is probably in your first 100 lines of Python code you ever wrote as shown in code snippet 5.8.

```
with open("rabbit.txt", 'w') as fp:
    fp.write("Hello, rabbit!")
```

CODE 5.8 A simplest context manager in Python.

Whatever you do inside the with statement won't affect the closing of the file because it is guaranteed that the file object `fp` will do some cleaning up after you are done with the reading and writing.

The file object `fp` is a context manager because it implements the following two dunder methods: __ *enter* __ () and __ *exit* __ (). The former is called to prepare the context and resources and the latter is called when the execution exits the with statement, as the name suggests.

Let's build our own *CoachContextManager* class to make sure our athletes warm up and relax properly (code snippet 5.9).

```
class CoachContextManager:
    def __init__(self):
        return
```

```
    def __enter__(self):
        print("Warm up for 20 minutes.")

    def __exit__(self, exc_type, exc_val, exc_tb):
        print("Stretch for 10 minutes.")


with CoachContextManager() as ccm:
    print("Play basketball for 40 minutes.")
```

CODE 5.9   The *CoachContextManager* class.

Run it. We do have a nice order structure as shown in log snippet 5.10.

```
Warm up for 20 minutes.
Play basketball for 40 minutes.
Stretch for 10 minutes.
```

CODE 5.10   The coach ensures warming up and cooling down.

Does the pattern look familiar? It feels like you as the coach are working as a coroutine: to warm them up. However, you release the autonomy of the athlete's bodies and let them play for a while as if it is another coroutine taking over the control. After they are done, you resume the execution: to help them stretch and relax.

In Figure 5.1, we can see how the athlete's CPU occupation is transferred between the coach and the athlete. This naturally mirrors a yield syntax. Is that possible that we rewrite the context manager using the yield syntax?

Yes. This is exactly what the *contextmanager* decorator from the *contextlib* module does. We can get rid of the class initiation. Instead, we simply decorate a function to turn it into a context manager.

Code snippet 5.10 is equivalent to the following *contextmanager* decorator version (code snippet 5.11).

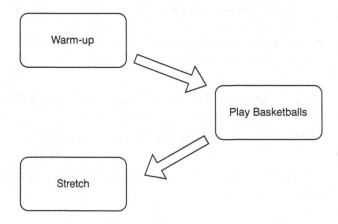

FIGURE 5.1   Context management as a yielding process.

```
from contextlib import contextmanager

@contextmanager
def coach():
    print("Warm up for 20 minutes.")
    yield
    print("Stretch for 10 minutes.")

with coach() as cmm:
    print("Play basketball for 40 minutes")
```

CODE 5.11   Use contextmanager to rewrite 5.10.

In the `coach()` function, whatever is before the *yield* is considered the equivalent of __ *enter* __ *()* method and whatever is after that is the equivalent of the __*exit*__ *()* method.

In fact, we can also make a context manager async. There is nothing fancy. Being async simply means a progress can be paused and resumed. An async context manager can pause its __*enter*__ *()* part or the __*exit*__ *()* part so some other work can be done. To distinguish the differences, async context manager will implement the __*aenter*__ *()* and the __*aexit*__ *()* methods. Without surprise, we have the *asynccontextmanager* decorator.

Suppose the coach needs to discuss the game strategy while warming up the team. Code snippet 5.12 simulates it.

```
import asyncio
from contextlib import asynccontextmanager

@asynccontextmanager
async def coach():
    print("Starting Warming Up")
    await asyncio.sleep(1)
    print("Warm up finish")
    try:
        yield
    finally:
        print("Starting stretching")
        await asyncio.sleep(1)
        print("Stretching is completed")

async def drunk_coach():
    async with coach() as ccm:
        print("Playing basketball!")

async def coach_talking():
    print("Coach is planing the game strategy")
    await asyncio.sleep(0.5)
```

```
async def main():
    await asyncio.gather(drunk_coach(), coach_talking())

if __name__ == "__main__":
    asyncio.run(main())
```

CODE 5.12   An asynchronous context manager example

Run it and we can see in the log snippet 5.13 that the drunk coach gives a speech during the warmup. The asynchronous context manager allows the coach to do so.

```
Starting Warming Up
Coach is planing the game strategy
Warm up finish
Playing basketball!
Starting stretching
Stretching is completed
```

CODE 5.13   The coach gives a speech during warmup.

The moral of the story is that a function can have a lot of externalities. To handle those externalities, a context manager is introduced to ensure that a function can restore its environment to what it was before the function runs. This is very important. For example, if you host a database and allow others to connect to it. If your developer kit doesn't automatically disconnect the connection when the users are done, you will risk overwhelming your own services.

Now, we have enough knowledge to dive into the big example: how to wrap a synchronous service so it is asynchronous with minimal syntax change.

DIVE INTO THE AIOSQLITE EXAMPLE

SQLite is a popular lightweight and serverless relational database management system that stores data in a single file on disk. It is so simple that developers love it to test proof of concepts. You don't need to manage a server, set up a client, etc.

The Python standard library includes the `sqlite3` module, which provides a simple and convenient way to interact with SQLite databases using Python. Code snippet 5.14 is a typical example of using the `sqlite3` module to interact with a database on the disk.

```
import sqlite3
con = sqlite3.connect("movie.db")
cur = con.cursor()
cur.execute("CREATE TABLE movie(title, year, score)")
cur.execute("""
    INSERT INTO movie VALUES
        ('Monty Python and the Holy Grail', 1975, 8.2),
        ('Crouching Tiger, Hidden Dragon', 2000, 7.9)
""")
con.commit()
```

```
for e in cur.execute("SELECT score FROM movie"):
    print(e)
```

CODE 5.14   Use vanilla `sqlite3` module in Python.

The synchronous code follows the following pattern. I am assuming that you are somewhat familiar with it, but it doesn't hurt much if not.

1. Connect to a database to obtain a connection object.

2. Acquire a cursor object to run queries.

3. Execute a query and obtain the results.

4. Repeat step 4.

To turn the code async is to enable several queries to run at the same time. Let's brainstorm the design before diving into the real implementation by Amethyst Reese.[2]

Based on our earlier experience, the first data structure we need to implement somewhere is a queue structure so we can store the queries to run without losing them. Since we want async execution, each query should correspond to a future that can be awaited for.

When we have a queue of queries, we need to pipe them into an executor so the executor can run them and fulfill the futures. In this case, an ideal executor is a thread. The execution at this level is synchronous but users won't notice it.

If possible, we also want to enable the usage of a connection as an asynchronous context manager, so it automatically closes when everything is done. Similarly, we want the cursor to become an async iterator, like the iterating of the synchronous result for the native version, but asynchronously.

Connection as an Executor and a Scheduler

There are two core objects in the implementation of aiosqlite: connection and cursor. Let's look at the *Connection* class first.

The *Connection* class inherits from *Thread*, so it has the *start()* and the *run()* methods naturally. This makes a connection a heavy-lifting executor naturally. Let's look at its central attributes first in snippet 5.15. I removed some boring stuff but if you are interested, you can check its source code in the *core.py*[3] file.

```
class Connection(Thread):
    def __init__(
        self,
        connector: Callable[[], sqlite3.Connection],
    ) -> None:
        self._connection: Optional[sqlite3.Connection] = None
        self._connector = connector
        self._tx: Queue = Queue()
```

CODE 5.15   The `Connection` class

The typing in this source code is amazing. A *Connection* instance is initialized with a connector, which is a *Callable*, likely a function, that takes no arguments but returns a real sqlite3 connection. It is then assigned to the _ *connector* attribute.

The _ *tx* is the queue that we were talking about. We will see what it does in the methods.

Let's check when the tasks get scheduled. We are looking for the keyword put as it is the way to push stuff into the queue. If you search put, you will find two interesting methods.

First, the _ execute() method in snippet 5.16.

```python
async def _execute(self, fn, *args, **kwargs):
    """Queue a function with the given arguments for execution."""
    if not self._running or not self._connection:
        raise ValueError("Connection closed")

    function = partial(fn, *args, **kwargs)
    future = asyncio.get_event_loop().create_future()

    self._tx.put_nowait((future, function))

    return await future
```

CODE 5.16   The _ execute() method.

The method first checks whether there is a valid connection and whether the thread is running. If Yes, it first packages the fn function with its argument to a new function called function using the partial methods. After that, it grabs a future from the air and puts the tuple (future, function) into the queue. Finally, wait for it.

What the *partial* function does is to fix certain arguments of a multiple-argument function to create a new function, so we don't need to pass arguments around in an error-prone way. Take code snippet 5.17 as an example, let's say you have a function to calculate the price after a discount, but you now want to expose a new function that fixes the discount at 30%.

```python
from functools import partial

def cal_price(discount, price):
    return price * (1-discount)

cal_price_3 = partial(cal_price, 0.3)

cal_price_3(10) # 7
```

CODE 5.17   functools.partial example.

partial is a powerful decorator that can encapsulate information within a function that you don't want the users to modify. However, most asyncio scheduling functions don't accept keyword arguments.

Like the _ *execute()* method, the _ *connect()* method is also utilizing the _ *tx* task queue to establish the connection. This explains why the _ *connector* attribute is a *Callable*, rather than a pre-created connection (code snippet 5.18). The interface for all tasks is universal, even when the task is to establish a connection.

```python
async def _connect(self) -> "Connection":
    """Connect to the actual sqlite database."""
    if self._connection is None:
        try:
            future = asyncio.get_event_loop().create_future()
            self._tx.put_nowait((future, self._connector))
            self._connection = await future
        except Exception:
            self._running = False
            self._connection = None
            raise

    return self
```

CODE 5.18 _ *connect()* is also considered a task put in the queue.

Next, let's move on to the task consumer. The key string we should be searching for is _ *tx.get()* as this is the way to fetch elements from a queue. This leads to the *run()* method, an overwriting of the *Thread.run()* method. Code snippet 5.19 removes some logging statements.

```python
def run(self) -> None:
    """
    Execute function calls on a separate thread.
    :meta private:
    """
    while True:
        try:
            future, function = self._tx.get(timeout=0.1)
        except Empty:
            if self._running:
                continue
            break
        try:
            result = function()
            def set_result(fut, result):
                if not fut.done():
                    fut.set_result(result)
            get_loop(future).call_soon_threadsafe(set_result,
future, result)
        except BaseException as e:
```

```
def set_exception(fut, e):
    if not fut.done():
        fut.set_exception(e)
get_loop(future).call_soon_threadsafe(set_exception,
future, e)
```

CODE 5.19   The *run()* method consumes tasks from the queue.

As long as there are queries to be completed, the *Connection*, a subclass of *Thread*, will pop tasks from the queue and try to run it. If the run is successful, it sets the future's result which also automatically marks the future as done, otherwise it sets an exception to the future.

The interesting thing here is the usage of the *call_soon_threadsafe()* function. It enforces that the task passed to it will run in a thread safe way. In other words, it ensures that the future will be set properly.

To understand why we need to check how this was done earlier. Before PR #15[4] back in 2018, there was a task queue *_tx* and a result queue *_rx*. When the thread grabs a task and runs it, it puts the result back into the result queue in the order the task is processed.

Recall that Python a *Queue* object is shared between threads. Multiple coroutines can put results into it. This causes an issue: how do we make sure that the order of the query results agrees with the order of the queries created?

Before PR #15, the *run()* method is unaware of who is waiting for the result. The problem was solved in a blunt way: the *_execute()* method implements a lock to ensure that the execution of a query and the returning of the query from the result queue is undisturbed. If there is no result in the result queue, it will just keep quickly polling the queue until the task completes. This clearly causes a potential performance issue.

To fix this, the contributor removed the result queue and the lock. Instead, let Python itself take care of the thread safety by calling standard library functions. This is a beautiful pull request.

Here is a quick summary of what we have figured out.

1. A real sqlite3 connection is wrapped with a *Connection* class instance which inherits a *Thread* object.

2. The *Connection* class, when started, will keep fetching queued tasks and execute them. This process is synchronous. However, the future's result setting is scheduled by an event loop. The asynchronous *_execute()* method will await for the future's finalization and return to the caller.

Connection and Cursor as Async Context Managers

For most other *Connection* methods, they are just mirroring of the sqlite3 counterparts. However, there are a few special ones.

The *Connection* class implements the __aenter__ () and the __aexit__ () dunder methods which makes it an asynchronous context manager. The syntax in snippet 5.20 therefore becomes legal.

```
async with aiosqlite.connect("movie_async.db") as db:
    # do stuff
```

CODE 5.20   Asynchronous context manager for establishing a connection.

This simple syntax involves a series of delegation.

1. First, the *connect()* function returns a *Connection* instance.

2. The __*aenter*__ *()* is called which invokes the __*await*__ *()* method.

3. In the __*await*__ *()* method, the thread starts which further calls the *_connect()* method.

4. The *_connect()* method, as we discussed earlier, creates the task to establish a real connection, and returns it to the hands of the user as db.

This concludes our analysis of the *Connection* class. How about the *Cursor*?

In vanilla sqlite3 code, code snippet 5.21 will return an error as a cursor cannot be used as a context manager.

```
with sqlite3.connect("movie.db") as con:
    with con.cursor() as cur:
        # AttributeError: __enter__
```

CODE 5.21   A vanilla sqlite3 cursor is not a context manager.

This means that a cursor is not a context manager. However, the aiosqlite allows syntax in snippet 5.22 which indicates that cursor itself is an asynchronous context manager.

```
async with aiosqlite.connect("movie.db") as db:
    async with db.cursor() as cursor:
        # do stuff
```

CODE 5.22   aiosqlite cursor is an asynchronous context manager.

What's more, snippet 5.23 also shows that a *Cursor* is also an asynchronous iterator.

```
async with aiosqlite.connect("movie.db") as db:
    async with db.execute("SELECT * FROM movie") as cursor:
        async for row in cursor:
            print(row)
```

CODE 5.23   *Cursor* is also an asynchronous iterator.

How is this possible?

Let's check the first case first. What does the *cursor()* method of the *Connection* class do? The *cursor()* method returns a *Cursor* object but the *Cursor* object's argument, a real sqlite3 connection cursor, is not immediately available which should be awaited for (code snippet 5.24).

```python
@contextmanager
async def cursor(self) -> Cursor:
    """Create an aiosqlite cursor wrapping a sqlite3 cursor
object."""
    return Cursor(self, await self._execute(self._conn.cursor))
```

CODE 5.24   The *cursor()* method returns a *Cursor* object.

Or Is it? let's check the definition of the *@contextmanager*. Note that this is not the contextlib contextmanager as we didn't import it. Sometimes it gets overwritten (code snippet 5.25).

```python
def contextmanager(
    method: Callable[..., Coroutine[Any, Any, _T]]
) -> Callable[..., Result[_T]]:
    @wraps(method)
    def wrapper(self, *args, **kwargs) -> Result[_T]:
        return Result(method(self, *args, **kwargs))

    return wrapper
```

CODE 5.25   Definition of @contextmanager.

The contextmanager function takes a callable called *method* and returns another callable called *wrapper*. Go over the source code; you will find the @contextmanager decorator always decorates methods, so the argument name is perfect.

Here, the *Callable[..., Coroutine[Any, Any, _T]]* typing means that it is a callable that takes arbitrary input but returns a coroutine. This agrees with the return of *cursor()* method as it still has an incomplete argument cursor.

However, after the decoration, we have a new callable that returns not a coroutine, but a *Result* class type (code snippet 5.26). So, what is a *Result*?

```python
class Result(AsyncContextManager[_T], Coroutine[Any, Any, _T]):
    __slots__ = ("_coro", "_obj")

    def __init__(self, coro: Coroutine[Any, Any, _T]):
        self._coro = coro
        self._obj: _T

    def send(self, value) -> None:
        return self._coro.send(value)

    def throw(self, typ, val=None, tb=None) -> None:
        if val is None:
            return self._coro.throw(typ)
```

```
        if tb is None:
            return self._coro.throw(typ, val)

        return self._coro.throw(typ, val, tb)

    def close(self) -> None:
        return self._coro.close()

    def __await__(self) -> Generator[Any, None, _T]:
        return self._coro.__await__()

    async def __aenter__(self) -> _T:
        self._obj = await self._coro
        return self._obj

    async def __aexit__(self, exc_type, exc, tb) -> None:
        if isinstance(self._obj, Cursor):
            await self._obj.close()
```

CODE 5.26   Result implements several protocols.

The `Result` class implements the protocols of both an asynchronous context manager as well as a coroutine. It is a coroutine so it can be awaited for. It is an asynchronous context manager so it can be asynchronously entered and exited.

When the `__aenter__ ()` is called, the `_coro` coroutine is awaited and assigned to `_obj`, which is further returned. This simplifies the async with statement as stated in PR #5, more specifically this commit: Make cursors usable as context managers without awaiting. This is also a beautiful pull request.

Let's summarize what we discussed so far.

1. The Cursor class is a wrapper of a real sqlite3 cursor.

2. When created using `cursor()` method, it is decorated by a contextmanager which makes the decorated *Result* an asynchronous context manager.

There is a small detail that we didn't cover. In the `contextmanager()` function, what does the `@wraps(method)` do?

The `wraps()` function is a function from the functools module. It is also a decorator. However, it is special because it doesn't change the behavior of the wrapped function but carries over its metadata like function names, docstrings and parameter names, etc. This is helpful for debugging and introspection purposes. Code snippet 5.27 is an example.

```
from functools import wraps

def logger(func):
    def wrapper(*args, **kwargs):
```

```
            return func(*args, **kwargs)
        return wrapper

def logger_wrap(func):
    @wraps(func)
    def wrapper(*args, **kwargs):
        return func(*args, **kwargs)
    return wrapper

@logger
def add(a, b):
    return a + b

print(add.__name__)

@logger_wrap
def add(a, b):
    return a + b

print(add.__name__)
```

CODE 5.27   wraps carries metadata over to the decorated function.

The first add function's name is lost. Its name becomes "wrapper" while the second one's is preserved thanks to the wraps decorator.

At this stage, you probably understand why I excluded the synchronous to asynchronous example from the previous chapter. It is so complicated that it is simply impractical to throw so much content to my readers.

At the very end, let's look at how the delegation from the *Cursor* to the *Connection* is done, which echoes the usage of the partial decorator we introduced earlier.

Shown in snippet 5.28, the *execute()* method of the *Cursor* object will invoke its own _ *execute()* method.

```
async def execute(self, sql: str, parameters: Iterable[Any] =
None) -> "Cursor":
    """Execute the given query."""
    if parameters is None:
        parameters = []
    await self._execute(self._cursor.execute, sql, parameters)
    return self
```

CODE 5.28   *execute()* invokes _ *execute()* method.

Which essentially delegates the execution to the *Connection* object's _ *execute()*.

```
async def _execute(self, fn, *args, **kwargs):
```

```
    """Execute the given function on the shared connection's
thread."""
    return await self._conn._execute(fn, *args, **kwargs)
```

CODE 5.29 *Connection's_ execute()* does the actual jobs.

So now we see what the partial function bundles together. It is the real sqlite3 cursor's *execute()* function, the sql query string and parameters if there are any.

By now, we covered the most important parts that aiosqlite implements. There are still tons of details in the source code. I would encourage you to read carefully yourself to appreciate its cleanliness and elegance.

SUMMARY

This chapter is about empowering Python functions so they can be enhanced or even enchanted. We started with a simple use case of retrying an unstable function, then discussed the concept of context manager, introduced decorator, etc. At the end, we discussed the wrapping of a synchronous library with asynchronous interfaces. This is not an easy task but if you made it this far, good job!

NOTES

1 https://github.com/rholder/retrying
2 https://github.com/amyreese
3 https://github.com/omnilib/aiosqlite/blob/main/aiosqlite/core.py
4 https://github.com/omnilib/aiosqlite/pull/15

## CHAPTER 6

Selected OOP Design Best Practices

UNDERSTAND YOUR BUSINESS

Before writing the first line of Python code, you should understand the business you are trying to model or emulate very well. This is especially true for object-oriented programming. If there are design flaws in object-oriented programming code and you provide them to users, it will take extra effort on the user's end to mitigate the damage and the mitigation is often error prone. Ultimately, the *complexity* of the codebase will become unmanageable. However, having a clean, reusable oriented-programming design will lower the barrier to understanding, remove obstacles to integrate the new code with existing code base and build robust and reliable applications.

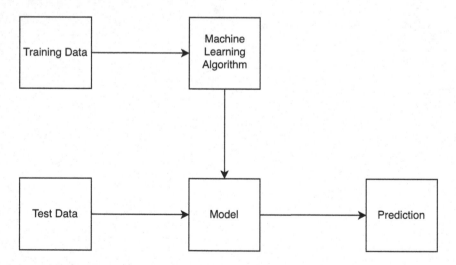

FIGURE 6.1   Basic machine learning flowchart.

DOI: 10.1201/9781003316909-7

In this chapter, we will study a well-designed Python library: scikit-learn. scikit-learn is a popular machine learning library that makes it super easy for programmers to build predictive models and perform data analysis and machine learning. It provides a set of tools for machine learning tasks, such as classification, regression, clustering and dimensionality reduction. Note that Scikit-learn is not the go-to library for deep learning and other neural-network-based tasks, at which PyTorch and TensorFlow do a better job.

A Quick Overview of *the* Business

Suppose this year is 2010 and you are thinking of developing a machine learning library. You have had enough of MATLAB or other shabby commercial software. How would you design the architecture of the library? Earlier we saw that in *aiosqlite*, the core classes are *Cursor* and *Connection*. What are our core classes for machine learning?

For readers who are not familiar with machine learning, here is a quick, incomplete introduction.

For *traditional* machine learning tasks, in contrast with deep learning, there are two common goals:

1. To find a relationship between the *features* and the *labels*.

2. Or to find structural characteristics in the unlabeled datasets.

The former is called supervised machine learning and the latter is called unsupervised machine learning.

An example for supervised machine learning is to create a model to predict the chance of having diabetes, given a set of features like eating habits, family diabetes history, exercising habits, etc.

An example of unsupervised machine learning is clustering. For example, there are a few movies with descriptions. A clustering algorithm should be able to group these movies into several categories.

The biggest difference between supervised learning and unsupervised learning is that supervised learning makes use of ground truth. To learn what features contribute to diabetes, we must know whether a person has diabetes or not beforehand. In other words, we need to have *labels*. Unsupervised learning aims to discover the characteristics of the feature set itself. For example, if two movies' descriptions both include the word "angel" then it may indicate that these two movies are like each other. However, we are never *certain* about this association as we don't have access to the ground truth.

For both types of algorithms, the following steps shown in Figure 6.1 are the most basic ones.

However, in real life, this workflow is too good to be true. For example, most training data are not suitable for machine learning algorithms to digest directly. Computers don't understand the word "angel" and we must use numerical values to represent them. Some features may be in the magnitude of thousands and others may be much smaller

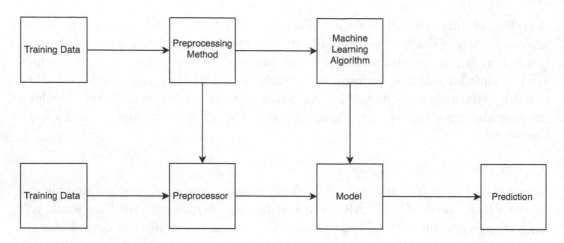

FIGURE 6.2   Preprocessing.

numerically. This makes distance calculation highly unstable, which is widely used in many unsupervised machine learning algorithms. We need to *normalize* the numerical values. Such a step is often called preprocessing. Then our workflow becomes something in Figure 6.2.

So, we use training data to create a preprocessor and use the same preprocessor to pre-process the test data. You may wonder why not use all the data. Isn't it more accurate? Not really. Using test data at any step in the training process, including data preprocessing has the risk of *data leaking*. No information from the testing data, even the range of the numerical values, should be allowed when we build the model.

Fair enough, but this is not the whole picture. There are other steps that are part of the flow chart. For example, cross-validation is a common practice when building a model: because machine learning models often have untrainable parameters, and we often don't know which set of parameters is better. Cross-validation allows us to evaluate the qualities of different models. It can also help us prevent the so-called overfitting.

Our pipeline becomes the following Figure 6.3.

Besides entities and processes in this pipeline, there are other entities we need to model. Metrics is one of them. We need metrics to measure how good a machine learning model is. For example, if the model predicts binary categories, the accuracy rate and F1 score are the go-to metrics. The dataset also needs to be modeled. We need a *unified* format of datasets so the digestion of datasets will follow a *unified* interface.

Before moving on, let's summarize what we try to achieve in our *business*.

1. Data needs to be preprocessed and separated into training sets and test sets.

2. A model needs to be built by something like a *model* factory using the training dataset.

3. Model selection like cross-validation needs to be integrated seamlessly.

Next, we will design our classes that enable such a *business*.

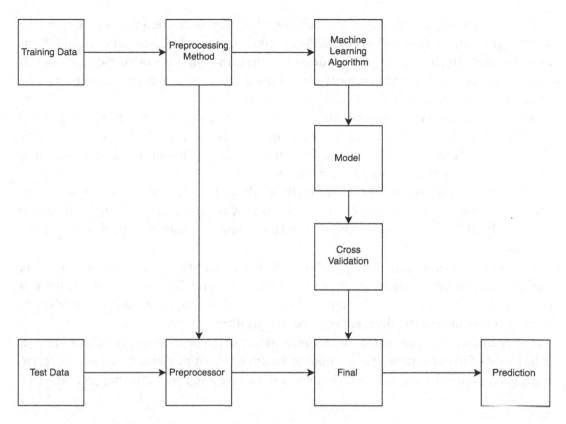

FIGURE 6.3 Machine learning pipelines with cross-validation.

MODEL THE BUSINESS ENTITIES WITH OOP

Design the Core Entities

First, the most important entities are the *machine learning algorithms* and *models*. Technically, the algorithm is a *factory* of the models. With the same algorithm but different parameters, we can produce a lot of copies of models.

However, if you think about it more carefully, this may not sound right. A model is created by training on a training dataset. This is a *continuous* process. Say I have 5000 rows of records in my training dataset. I trained a linear regression model using 2500 rows. I got a model called *lg_2500*. However, I am not done training, I need to finish training on the remaining 2500 rows to get *lg_5000*. This doesn't make sense as we literally created 5000 models during the process, even though we choose to *release* the final model only. This is just conceptually ugly.

Another drawback is the lack of ease of use. Say I pick up a serialized model, deserialize it as I want to continue improving it with recently available data. However, I got the model from another engineer, and he already left the company. I can't train the model as I can't find the factory that produces it. What if there are version issues (and there will be)? This is a nightmare.

In 2013, the paper API design for machine learning software: experiences from the scikit-learn project[1] covered how the APIs of scikit-learn are designed. API design reflects how the underlined core entities are designed. Even though it is not very explicit in this paper, I think the first and foremost important decision is to combine the *factory* of a model and the *model* itself. It is called an *estimator*.

We may think in two directions. First, an estimator is a model whose training algorithm is self-contained. Or an estimator is a training algorithm that binds the model it creates. From the perspective of the overall design, the first interpretation is more accurate. I may exchange the usage of *model* and *estimator* sometimes.

All estimators implement the `fit()` method. The `fit()` method, for supervised learning algorithms, has a signature `fit(X, y)` where X is the training features and y is the training label. The fit method returns the class itself as a trained model with learned parameters.

For most machine learning algorithms, there are hyperparameters whose values are pre-determined before training. Those parameters are initialized when the estimator is initialized in the `__init__()` method. Examples are like depth of a decision tree or the penalizing coefficients for different regression algorithms.

For example, code snippet 6.1 shows the signature of the `DecisionTreeClassifier`. It has a lot of hyperparameters and note some are not even numerical. A machine learning algorithm can have different variations and they are also considered hyperparameters.

```python
def __init__(
        self,
        *,
        criterion="gini",
        splitter="best",
        max_depth=None,
        min_samples_split=2,
        min_samples_leaf=1,
        min_weight_fraction_leaf=0.0,
        max_features=None,
        random_state=None,
        max_leaf_nodes=None,
        min_impurity_decrease=0.0,
        class_weight=None,
        ccp_alpha=0.0,
    ):
    pass
```

CODE 6.1 `DecisionTreeClassifier` initialization.

One reason scikit-learn is great is that it uses the *most sensible* defaults for hyperparameters whenever possible. Users don't need to unconfidently choose parameters. For most cases, the algorithm just works out of the box well.

For the learned parameters, they are determined during the call of the *fit()* method. Their values will depend on the datasets. Such parameters include coefficients in linear regression, splitting criteria in tree-based algorithms and all the parameters in neural networks. For architecture that powers state-of-art language models, there are thousands of billions of them.

For example, the *DecisionTreeClassifier*'s *fit()* falls back to the implementation[2] of its parent class *BaseDecisionTree*.

Naturally, besides the *fit()* method, the estimators must also have parameter-related utility methods like *get _ params()* and *set _ params()*. They are both implemented in the *BaseEstimator* class. For example, the parameters are stored as attributes of the estimator objects directly and can be retrieved as in code snippet 6.2.

```python
def get_params(self, deep=True):
    """
    Get parameters for this estimator.
    Parameters
    ----------
    deep : bool, default=True
        If True, will return the parameters for this estimator and
        contained subobjects that are estimators.
    Returns
    -------
    params : dict
        Parameter names mapped to their values.
    """
    out = dict()
    for key in self._get_param_names():
        value = getattr(self, key)
        if deep and hasattr(value, "get_params") and not
isinstance(value, type):
            deep_items = value.get_params().items()
            out.update((key + "__" + k, val) for k, val in
deep_items)
        out[key] = value
    return out
```

CODE 6.2   Implementation of *get _ params()*.

However, an estimator is not only for learning models. The idea of *fit* on data also applies to data preprocessing. For example, if I want to standardize the feature ranges using the *StandardScaler*,[3] we also need to know the maximum and the minimum of the feature and *fit* the rest of the data into this range.

However, *StandardScaler* is fundamentally different from a model as it still outputs the data, specifically, the transformed data. We call it a *Transformer*. A transformer is an entity that not only fits on data, but also transforms it. A transformer has another method called `transform()`. Let's look at `StandardScaler`'s transform method in code snippet 6.3.

```
def transform(self, X, copy=None):
    # skip
    if sparse.issparse(X):
        # skip
    else:
        if self.with_mean:
            X -= self.mean_
        if self.with_std:
            X /= self.scale_
    return X
```

CODE 6.3   Implementation of standardization.

The core logic is that if we want to centralize the data around its mean, we subtract the mean from everyone. If we want to *shrink* the values by a scale of standard deviation, we divide everyone by the standard deviation.

Besides the `transform()` method, transformer classes also implement the `fit_transform()` method that combines the fit and transform steps together.

The interesting thing is that there is no such class called `BaseTransformer`. There is only a real `BaseEstimator` class. We will discuss why in the next subsection. Let's look at the last core entity: predictors.

A `predictor` class is an estimator with prediction capacity. It has the `predict()` and `score()` methods. The former takes the test X and predicts the labels for them. Even for unsupervised machine learning algorithms like K means, whose `predict()` will produce the unordered cluster label as an integer index.

The `score()` method produces a numerical score that measures how good the prediction is. For classification problems, it quantifies the *discrepancy* between the predicted labels and the ground truth labels. For regression problems, it measures the *distance* between the predicted values and the ground truth values.

We now have three core entities. Their relationship looks like the following.

However, I mentioned earlier that there is no such thing called a `BaseTransformer` or a `BasePredictor` and the inheritance relationship shown in Figure 6.4 is never explicit in scikit-learn. What's going on?

Establish the Relationship between Classes

Instead of subclassing the `BaseEstimator` as a `Transformer` or `Predictor`, scikit-learn used mixin to *mix* some properties *in* the child. We will compare the differences between inheritance and mixin shortly.

The `base.py` file defines the following important mixins.

1. `ClassifierMixin`

2. `RegressorMixin`

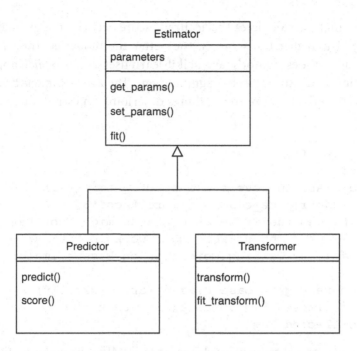

FIGURE 6.4   Core entities in scikit-learn.

3. ClusterMixin

4. DensityMixin

5. TransformerMixin

A mixin is just a class but it only adds the necessary flavor to the plate. For example, the *ClassifierMixin* defined in snippet 6.4 only has two methods: *score()* and _ *more _ tags()*.

```
class ClassifierMixin:
    """Mixin class for all classifiers in scikit-learn."""

    _estimator_type = "classifier"

    def score(self, X, y, sample_weight=None):
    # documentation skipped
        from .metrics import accuracy_score

        return accuracy_score(y, self.predict(X),
sample_weight=sample_weight)

    def _more_tags(self):
        return {"requires_y": True}
```

CODE 6.4   Definition of *ClassifierMixin*.

The *score()* method calculates the accuracy score between the ground truth and the predicted value. The higher the score is, the better the model is. The *_more_tags()* method adds a tag to the estimator's tags. scikit-learn uses a very *explicit* approach to identify the properties of an estimator: by tagging them. The *BaseEstimator* implemented a *_get_tags()* method that returns all tags describing an estimator as a set, as shown in snippet 6.5.

```
def _get_tags(self):
    collected_tags = {}
    for base_class in reversed(inspect.getmro(self.__class__)):
        if hasattr(base_class, "_more_tags"):
            # need the if because mixins might not have _more_tags
            # but might do redundant work in estimators
            # (i.e. calling more tags on BaseEstimator multiple
times)
            more_tags = base_class._more_tags(self)
            collected_tags.update(more_tags)
    return collected_tags
```

CODE 6.5   *tags* are used to identify classes as well. Mixin provides additional tags.

Back to the mixin topic. With mixin, a classifier will be a child of both *BaseEstimator* and *ClassifierMixin*. For example, the *DecisionTreeClassifier* inherits the *ClassifierMixin* and *BaseDecisionTree* (code snippet 6.6).

```
class DecisionTreeClassifier(ClassifierMixin, BaseDecisionTree):
    #pass
```

CODE 6.6   *DecisionTreeClassifier* parents.

The *BaseDecisionTree* is a child of the *BaseEstimator* and another mixin *MultiOutputMixin*. This mixin basically allows estimators to support multiple output like performing multiple category classification (code snippet 6.7).

```
class BaseDecisionTree(MultiOutputMixin, BaseEstimator,
metaclass=ABCMeta):
    #pass
```

CODE 6.7   *BaseDecisionTree* parents.

Why is this approach important? In our first lesson of OOP in college or on any OOP YouTube video, isn't the go-to relationship? Why don't we have something as in Figure 6.5?

The reason is that it is too easy to create a diamond structure with such multiple inheritances. A decision tree is a classifier, and it can output multiple labels. We then have the following inheritance relationship as in Figure 6.6.

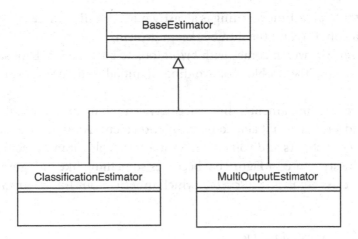

FIGURE 6.5   Inheritance from *BaseEstimator*.

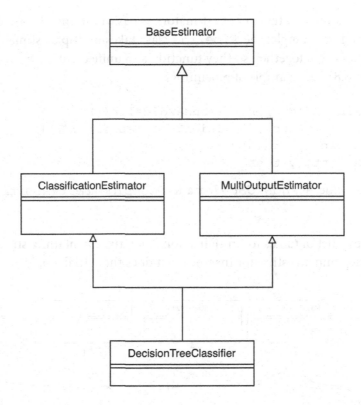

FIGURE 6.6   Diamond structure.

Now, if both *ClassifierEstimator* and *MultiOutputEstimator* implement the same method, which one should *DecisionTreeClassifier* inherit? Such confusion can be mitigated by carefully inspecting the *method resolution order* (MRO), but it creates an unnecessary mental burden to think about such a relationship all the time.

Most importantly, machine learning is a vastly huge domain. There are so many classes that scikit-learn contains and the number keeps growing.

If you use *pyreverse*, which comes with *pylint* tool, to build an UML for scikit-learn, you will see what I mean. The problem of avoiding diamond structure's side effects becomes impractical.

To summarize, the fundamental difference between mixin and multi-inheritance is that a mixin is an add-on that is not able to fully function alone. A mixin adds additional functionality to our *base* objects and you can move it around, plug it in to arbitrary classes like a Lego block. The structure in Figure 6.6 becomes something like in Figure 6.7. I included one *transformer* class `StandardScaler` which inherits from `BaseEstimator` and two other mixins.

The Benefits of Universal *interface*

Now, let's talk about some additional important *business* topics in machine learning besides the core entities.

There are estimators that take other estimators as basic building blocks. They are called meta-estimators. For example, the `Pipeline` class takes multiple estimators *in order* as input and bundles them together, so they function as a unified entity.

Code snippet 6.8 is an example of pipelining.

```
pipe = Pipeline([('scaler', StandardScaler()),
                 ('dtc', DecisionTreeClassifier())])
pipe.fit(X_train, y_train)
pipe.score(X_test, y_test)
```

CODE 6.8   Combine `StandardScaler` and `DecisionTreeClassifier` in a pipeline.

The pipe takes a list of tuples for initialization. Each tuple contains a string as the name of the current step and an estimator instance that does the actual job.

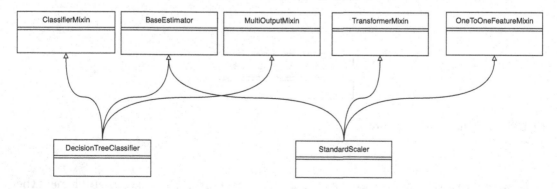

FIGURE 6.7   Mixin structure.

Pipeline *is* an estimator therefore it also implements the *fit()* method, which continuously calls each estimator in the line. If the last estimator in the pipe is a *predictor*, then Pipeline will also become a *predictor* with *score()* or *predict()* implemented.

What's super nice is that you can easily switch components of the pipeline. Let's say you think a single decision tree classifier is not enough, you want a forest (code snippet 6.9).

```
pipe = Pipeline([('scaler', StandardScaler()),
                 ('rfc', RandomForestClassifier())])
```

CODE 6.9   Switch the classifier from code snippet 6.8.

With such minimal code change, our code base will continue to work. This is a clear demonstration of the power of universal interface.

Let's look at a different meta-estimator: *GridSearchCV*. It is an estimator that takes another estimator and searches for the latter's best hyperparameters on a parameter space grid, using cross-validation (code snippet 6.10).

```
from sklearn import svm, datasets
from sklearn.model_selection import GridSearchCV
iris = datasets.load_iris()
parameters = {'kernel':('linear', 'rbf'), 'C':[1, 10]}
svc = svm.SVC()
clf = GridSearchCV(svc, parameters)
clf.fit(iris.data, iris.target)
```

CODE 6.10   An official example of *GridSearchCV*.

The estimator *SVC*, C-support vector machine classifier, is a classifier that utilizes a support vector machine, which is a once-super-hot machine learning model. The *C* here stands for penalization because people often use letter C to denote the penalizing coefficient.

Let's check the class' __init__ () method in code snippet 6.11.

```
def __init__(
      self,
      *,
      C=1.0,
      kernel="rbf",
      # skipped
)
```

CODE 6.11   Initialization of a support vector machine classifier.

Both *C* and *kernel* are pre-defined hyperparameters. The *GridSearchCV* basically takes the *parameters* and builds a 2 by 2 parameter space grid, in total 4 combinations, to find the best parameter set for the classifier.

To avoid overfitting, the model quality evaluation is done using cross-validation. The *iris* dataset is split into several *folds*, by default five. Four of them will be used for training and one for *validation*. This is repeated five times and the average is used for the final evaluation.

Like pipelining, the greatest thing about *GridSearchCV* is that you can easily plug in any estimator and provide a set of parameters and its choices. *GridSearchCV* will work out of the box. This is another advantage of the universal interface.

Even *GridSearchCV* itself is also an estimator. It has its own *fit()* method, so you attach it as the last stage of a pipeline.

Sometimes No OOP is the Best Design

Sometimes the best OOP design is to not have one. In scikit-learn, there are two examples.

Duck-typing may be more suitable than a rigorous inheritance relationship. scikit-learn supports duck-typing. Duck-typing is a programming concept in which the type or class of an object is less important than the set of methods and attributes it possesses. In other words, if an object walks like a duck and quacks like a duck, it's considered a duck, regardless of its actual type.

For example, when building pipelines or performing cross-validation, scikit-learn doesn't check the objects' type. Instead, it checks whether the class implements the necessary methods that an estimator or predictor *should* implement. In snippet 6.12, I created a silly estimator called *AllZeroEstimator*. Its only output is zero.

```python
class AllZeroEstimator:
    def __init__(self):
        pass
    def get_params(self, deep = True):
        return dict()
    def fit(self, X, y):
        pass
    def predict(self, X):
        return np.array([0 for _ in range(len(X.shape[0]))])
    def score(self, X, y):
        return 0
```

CODE 6.12   Create a new estimator called *AllZeroEstimator*.

However, I can plug it into a pipeline without any issue. Code snippet 6.13 is perfectly legal and runnable.

```python
from sklearn.datasets import load_iris
from sklearn.pipeline import Pipeline
from sklearn.preprocessing import StandardScaler
from sklearn.decomposition import PCA

iris = load_iris()

pipe_steps = [
    ('scaler', StandardScaler()),
```

```
    ('pca', PCA(n_components=2)),
    ('classifier', AllZeroEstimator())
]

pipe = Pipeline(pipe_steps)
```

CODE 6.13   Use *AllZeroEstimator* with scikit-learn pipelines.

This makes development and customization of scikit-learn very handy and friendly. Users can create their own estimator without inheriting the classes provided by the library.

In addition to duck-typing, scikit-learn made another important decision: no modeling for the dataset. It is completely up to the library users to make sure their dataset is tidy and well-formatted. In another word, there is no such a class called *BaseDataset* so users can inherit and model their data.

scikit-learn algorithms take plain NumPy arrays as input. This seems very trivial nowadays and has almost become a default truth not only for scikit-learn but for the whole machine learning ecosystem. However, if you look at scikit-learn's predecessors, people spend quite some time to get the dataset right.

In Weka, a statistical learning and data mining software, you must format your data as an Arff format. Arff stands for *Attribute-Relation File Format*. It is a text file that contains a lot of metadata. The famous iris dataset looks like snippet 6.14. Note that I already skipped a lot of information.

```
% 1. Title: Iris Plants Database
%
% 2. Sources:
%      (a) Creator: R.A. Fisher
%      (b) Donor: Michael Marshall (MARSHALL%PLU@io.arc.nasa.gov)
%      (c) Date: July, 1988
%
% 3. Past Usage:
%      - Publications: too many to mention!!!  Here are a few.
%      1. Fisher,R.A. "The use of multiple measurements in taxonomic
problems"
%         Annual Eugenics, 7, Part II, 179-188 (1936); also in
"Contributions
%         to Mathematical Statistics" (John Wiley, NY, 1950).
%
% 4. Relevant Information:
%      --- This is perhaps the best known database to be found in
the pattern
%
% 5. Number of Instances: 150 (50 in each of three classes)
%
% 6. Number of Attributes: 4 numeric, predictive attributes and
the class
%
% 7. Attribute Information:
```

```
%     1. sepal length in cm
%
% 8. Missing Attribute Values: None
%
% Summary Statistics:
%                  Min  Max   Mean    SD   Class Correlation
%     sepal length: 4.3  7.9   5.84  0.83    0.7826
% 9. Class Distribution: 33.3% for each of 3 classes.

@RELATION iris

@ATTRIBUTE sepallength   REAL
@ATTRIBUTE sepalwidth    REAL
@ATTRIBUTE petallength   REAL
@ATTRIBUTE petalwidth    REAL
@ATTRIBUTE class   {Iris-setosa,Iris-versicolor,Iris-virginica}

@DATA
5.1,3.5,1.4,0.2,Iris-setosa
4.9,3.0,1.4,0.2,Iris-setosa
```

CODE 6.14   The iris dataset in the Arff format.

This text file is essentially a class. The class has attributes like *title*, *sources* and *number of instances*, etc. Although not all fields are necessary, you still need to meet the minimum requirements for Weka to read it.

In scikit-learn, none of the information is needed. If the user wants to know how many attributes are there, just check the *shape* of the input *X*. In my opinion, this significantly increased the popularity of scikit-learn. When you run a SQL query to obtain a tabular dataset or convert an Excel file to a csv file, scikit-learn will just read it without asking you to provide more information. The implicit agreement between the user and the library creator is awesome: we do what we are supposed to do well, respectively.

To clarify that I am not criticizing any other software or libraries. The development of statistical learning tools has its own historical footprints. For example, Weka was originally developed in the 1990s while numpy was first available in the 2000s.

SUMMARY

In this chapter, we used scikit-learn as an example to talk about how object-oriented programming is utilized. We covered the goals that the library tries to achieve, the design of the core entities and their relationships. We also demonstrated several benefits brought by the design choices of scikit-learn. In the end, we covered some duck typing and a special case that OOP is not always the best option for the development of a library or an ecosystem.

NOTES

1 https://arxiv.org/abs/1309.0238
2 https://github.com/scikit-learn/scikit-learn/blob/main/sklearn/tree/_classes.py#L177
3 https://github.com/scikit-learn/scikit-learn/blob/main/sklearn/preprocessing/_data.py#L659

## CHAPTER 7

Testing in a Pistachio Shell

INTRODUCTION

This is the last chapter of this book. The chapter topic is testing. I put testing at the end of this book not because it is unimportant, but because it is so important that I hope readers have a good grasp of concepts like decorators and attribute lookup to fully appreciate the testing techniques. Those concepts are covered in earlier chapters. If you don't know them, I would suggest you read corresponding chapters first. If you do, we can start.

Like other chapters, I will assume that you have a rough idea of what testing is. There are three most common Python testing frameworks: unittest, pytest and doctest. We will focus on the unittest and pytest. Instead of turning this chapter into a hands-on tutorial, let's focus on *ideas* that are universal in both libraries rather than *syntax* differences.

FIXTURE AND PARAMETERIZATION

Let's say you wrote a function to find all the prime factors of a number. It looks like code snippet 7.1. We want to ensure its correctness.

```python
class PrimeFactorizer:
    def __init__(self):
        pass

    def prime_factors(self, n):
        factors = []
        i = 2
        while i * i <= n:
            if n % i:
                i += 1
            else:
                n //= i
                factors.append(i)
```

DOI: 10.1201/9781003316909-8

```
if n > 1:
    factors.append(n)
return factors
```

CODE 7.1   Plain implementation to find all prime factors.

First, let me briefly introduce what the *prime_factors()* method does. Any positive integer greater than 1 can be decomposed as a product of prime numbers. A prime number is a number that can only be decomposed as a product of 1 and itself, no other options. For example, 5 is a prime number but 6 is not: 6 equals 3 times 2. After it, 7, 11 and 13 are also prime numbers. The prime numbers are more and more sparse but there are infinitely many of them.

A fundamental theorem in number theory is that all non-prime numbers are products of prime numbers. For example, 72 is a product of 2, 2, 2, 3 and 3. This is somewhat easy for small numbers but can be notoriously difficult for large numbers. In the code above, we have the naivest way to find them.

Starting at 2, and capped by the square root of the input value, we divide the input value by 2, 3, etc. If there is an exact division, we take the quotient to repeat the process.

Let's manually try a number, say 70.

The number 2 divides 70 so the first number is 2 and the quotient is 35; 3 doesn't divide 35 but 5 does. Therefore, the second prime number is 5. The quotient is 7; 7 divides 7 and the quotient is 1. The code does a few more *useless* loops and stops. We have our final list 2, 5 and 7.

Let's write some tests. I put code snippet 7.1 into a file called *prime_factorizer.py* and code snippet 7.2 into a file called *test_ prime _ factorizer.py.* They are in the same folder.

```
import pytest

from prime_factorizer import PrimeFactorizer

class TestPrimeFactorizer:
    def test_prime_factors(self):
        factorizer = PrimeFactorizer()
        assert factorizer.prime_factors(12) == [2, 2, 3]
        assert factorizer.prime_factors(84) == [2, 2, 3, 7]
        assert factorizer.prime_factors(1024) == [2] * 10
        assert factorizer.prime_factors(1) == []
        assert factorizer.prime_factors(2) == [2]
        assert factorizer.prime_factors(7919) == [7919]
        assert factorizer.prime_factors(123456789) == [3, 3, 3607,
3803]
```

CODE 7.2   Test the *prime _ factors()* method.

It looks like we write some pretty good edge cases. We can run the test by typing the command in snippet 7.3 in the terminal.

```
python3 -m pytest test_prime_factorizer.py
```

CODE 7.3 Run the test from command line.

The test passed successfully.

Parameterization

Everything looks good so far. However, we would love to *extract* the inputs and expected outputs out of the *test_prime_factors()* method. This *separates* the data and the test so we can write more concise and readable test code by avoiding duplication and increasing flexibility.

To parametrize a test function, in code snippet 7.4 we use the *@pytest.mark. parametrize* decorator.

```
class TestPrimeFactorizer:
    @pytest.mark.parametrize("n, expected_factors", [
        (12, [2, 2, 3]),
        (84, [2, 2, 3, 7]),
        (1024, [2] * 10),
        (1, []),
        (2, [2]),
        (7919, [7919]),
        (123456789, [3, 3, 3607, 3803]),
    ])
    def test_prime_factors(self, n, expected_factors):
        factorizer = PrimeFactorizer()
        assert factorizer.prime_factors(n) == expected_factors
```

CODE 7.4 Parameterize the test inputs and outputs.

The decorator takes a string that indicates the names of the inputs and the outputs. Then we feed a list of tuples to it, each as an input and output pair.

Run the test again, instead of 1 test, this time pytest picks up 7 tests. Each pair of input and output essentially creates a new test as shown in code snippet 7.5. You can also assign ids to a specific test, so it is easy to trace them if something goes wrong. You can simply put *-v* in the pytest command to show the verbose information.

```
class TestPrimeFactorizer:
    @pytest.mark.parametrize("n, expected_factors", [
        (12, [2, 2, 3]),
        (84, [2, 2, 3, 7]),
```

```
            (1024, [2] * 10),
            (1, [],),
            (2, [2]),
            (7919, [7919]),
            (123456789, [3, 3, 3607, 3803]),
    ], ids=["12", "84", "1024", "1", "2", "7919", "123456789"])
    def test_prime_factors(self, n, expected_factors):
        factorizer = PrimeFactorizer()
        assert factorizer.prime_factors(n) == expected_factors
```

CODE 7.5   Add identifiers to each parameter set.

Now, suppose the user of this function is not very good at math. The guy will likely throw data other than positive integers into this function. How should we guard against it? In other words, we want to make sure our function fails properly through testing.

In tests, sometimes we not only want to ensure success, but we also want to ensure failure. In code snippet 7.6, let's see how requests[1] handle the case when users provide a wrong URL for it to query.

```
@pytest.mark.parametrize(
    "exception, url",
    (
            (MissingSchema, "hiwpefhipowhefopw"),
            (InvalidSchema, "localhost:3128"),
            (InvalidSchema, "localhost.localdomain:3128/"),
            (InvalidSchema, "10.122.1.1:3128/"),
            (InvalidURL, "http://"),
            (InvalidURL, "http://*example.com"),
            (InvalidURL, "http://.example.com"),
    ),
)
def test_invalid_url(self, exception, url):
    with pytest.raises(exception):
        requests.get(url)
```

CODE 7.6   Requests use parameterization to test different errors.

This set of tests test 3 cases with the proper error message. Normally, *pytest.raises* returns an object of type *RaisesContext*, which is a context manager that will make sure the inner operation will raise the assigned exception.

In our case, we need to modify the *prime _ factors()* method first. Let's add two error checks at the beginning as shown in snippet 7.7.

```
def prime_factors(self, n):
    if not isinstance(n, int):
        raise TypeError("Input must be an integer")
```

```
if n < 1:
    raise ValueError("Input must be a positive integer")
#skip
```

CODE 7.7 Add two checks in *prime_factors()*.

Then we can write a test to make sure the method fails when it is supposed to.

```
@pytest.mark.parametrize("n, expected_error", [
    (-1, ValueError),
    (0, ValueError),
    (1.2, TypeError),
    ("string", TypeError),
    (None, TypeError)
])
def test_prime_factors_errors(self, n, expected_error):
    factorizer = PrimeFactorizer()
    with pytest.raises(expected_error):
        factorizer.prime_factors(n)
```

CODE 7.8 Ensure that proper errors are raised in the test.

Run the code and we do see that the test is passed which means the exact errors are raised (code snippet 7.8).

Resources and Fixture

Did you smell something that is not DRY? DRY here means *don't repeat yourself*. In both tests, we create an instance of *PrimeFactorizer*. Can we remove such redundancy? This may not become an obvious issue when we only have a handful of tests. However, if there are thousands of tests and we are changing the instance creation, we may run into hidden mines.

The way to solve this issue is to build the processes of resource preparation and resource teardown. As a general principle of testing, in order to run a test, we may need to provide some resources for it to run, when the test is done, we tear down the resources as if *nothing* happens. Sometimes this is harder than you think. We will have to create artificial environments to *fool* the test. This is the topic of the next section.

In the pytest framework, this is done by introducing a fixture.

We define a fixture called *factorizer()* that returns a new instance of the PrimeFactorizer class. We then pass this fixture as an argument to both test methods, which allows us to simplify the setup code in each test (code snippet 7.9).

```
@pytest.fixture
def factorizer():
    return PrimeFactorizer()


# skip
```

```
def test_prime_factors_errors(self, factorizer, n,
expected_error):
    with pytest.raises(expected_error):
        factorizer.prime_factors(n)
```

CODE 7.9 Use a fixture to create the *PrimeFactorizer* instance.

Note that each test, corresponding to each pair of input and output, will have their independent *PrimeFactorizer* instance. Add some printing in the *factorizer()* function and add *-s* in the command when running the test, we will see that the instances are independent.

We can achieve something similar in the unittest framework. Instead of using a fixture, unittest provides some name-fixed methods to prepare the test classes. The most common two are *setUp()* and *tearDown()* (code snippet 7.10).

```
import unittest
from prime_factorizer import PrimeFactorizer

class TestPrimeFactorizer(unittest.TestCase):
    def setUp(self):
        self.factorizer = PrimeFactorizer()

    def tearDown(self):
        self.factorizer = None
    # skip
```

CODE 7.10 unittest uses *setUp()* and *tearDown()* methods to prepare and destroy resources.

Then for each test, this pair of methods will be called before and after respectively. This is exactly like a context manager: we halt the resource management coroutine, run the test, then hand over the execution right for the resource management to complete.

Let's see an example of using *setUp()* and *tearDown()* in aiosqlite. In the smoke.py[2] file, before running every test, the old database file will be deleted if it exists (code snippet 7.11).

```
@classmethod
def setUpClass(cls):
    setup_logger()


def setUp(self):
    if TEST_DB.exists():
        TEST_DB.unlink()
```

```
def tearDown(self):
    if TEST_DB.exists():
        TEST_DB.unlink()
```

CODE 7.11 Smoke test in aiosqlite uses *setUp()* and *tearDown()*.

> A side note on smoke test: smoke test is an initial test designed to quickly determine if a system or application can function at a basic level. The term "smoke test" comes from the electronics industry, where technicians would test a new piece of equipment by turning it on and watching for smoke, as smoke would indicate that something had gone wrong.

Here we also see a new class method *setUpClass()*. It only runs once for all the test methods under a test class. Its effect will last for the whole life cycle of the class, rather than specific methods. Here it sets up a logger which makes sense.

MONKEY PATCH

Now, we have ensured that our *prime_factors()* works properly. Let's say you want to use this code in educational software. It needs to print out the result on the screen so students can see the results. Of course, in real life there should be an API that handles all outputs, etc. The idea here is that you want to access the *print()* function in a test environment to ensure it works properly. If you are testing on a virtual machine without a screen, how should you test it?

This is a typical situation with huge implications: some resources are just not accessible or too expensive to test. Examples include running a test against some external APIs and they are rate-limited or expensive, or testing some plotting libraries to ensure certain behaviors without a human checking.

We need monkey patching. In Python, monkey patching refers to the process of dynamically modifying a class or module at runtime, by replacing attributes or methods with new implementations. This technique can be used to modify the behavior of existing code without changing the source code.

Monkey patching is *dangerous* and should be avoided in production code. It often implies bad object-oriented programming designs, misaligned code versioning or lack of maintenance, etc. However, monkey patching is also a powerful technique that can be used for testing and debugging.

Modify the Built-in Print

Let's dynamically modify the *print()* function's behavior. Let's redirect the normal system standard output to a variable.

First, we print out the factorization results in the *prime_factors()* method as shown in code snippet 7.12. Since we dynamically change the value of *n* so we need to memorize it.

```
class PrimeFactorizer:
    def __init__(self):
        pass

    def prime_factors(self, n):
        m = n
        # skip
        print(f"Prime factors of {m} are {factors}")
        return factors
```

CODE 7.12   Print out the information in *prime_factors()* method.

Then we replace the built-in print with our new print: basically, append whatever is going to be printed to a list (code snippet 7.13).

```
class TestPrimeFactorizer:
    @pytest.fixture
    def mock_print(self, monkeypatch):
        output = []

        def mock_printer(*args, **kwargs):
            output.append(args[0])

        monkeypatch.setattr("builtins.print", mock_printer)

        return output

    @pytest.mark.parametrize("n, expected_factors", [
        (12, [2, 2, 3]),
        (84, [2, 2, 3, 7]),
        (1024, [2] * 10),
        (1, [],),
        (2, [2]),
        (7919, [7919]),
        (123456789, [3, 3, 3607, 3803]),
    ], ids=["12", "84", "1024", "1", "2", "7919", "123456789"])
    def test_prime_factors(self, n, expected_factors,
mock_print):
        factorizer = PrimeFactorizer()
        assert factorizer.prime_factors(n) == expected_factors
        assert f"Prime factors of {n} are {expected_factors}" in
mock_print
```

CODE 7.13   Monkey patch the print destination to a list.

The *mock _ print* maintains a list to store the printed arguments. The *mock _ printer()* function replaces the *builtins* module's default *print* function.

What is *builtins?* Every time you start a Python program, Python will import some functions or classes that you can use out of the box. They are shipped together with Python in a module named builtins. You can run *dir(__builtin __)* to examine the built-in functions, errors, etc. *print()* is one of them.

The builtins module behaves like a class object with attributes, therefore *monkeypatch* can dynamically set its attribute with the *setattr()* method. Then in and only in the test function that uses the *mock _ print* fixture, the system standard output becomes a list!

More Powerful Monkey Patching

The *monkeypatch* in pytest can do much more. Let's look at its usage in two famous open source libraries. flask[3] is a very popular light-weight web framework written in Python. Let's see what kind of fixtures it defines in its conftest.py[4] file. We will also pick up some additional tips along the way.

First, monkeypatch can change the environment variable. The fixture in snippet 7.14 will be created only once for the whole test session according to the decorator's argument. This fixture will also be *automatically* used for every test.

```
@pytest.fixture(scope="session", autouse=True)
def _standard_os_environ():
    mp = monkeypatch.MonkeyPatch()
    out = (
        (os.environ, "FLASK_ENV_FILE", monkeypatch.notset),
        (os.environ, "FLASK_APP", monkeypatch.notset),
        (os.environ, "FLASK_DEBUG", monkeypatch.notset),
        (os.environ, "FLASK_RUN_FROM_CLI", monkeypatch.notset),
        (os.environ, "WERKZEUG_RUN_MAIN", monkeypatch.notset),
    )

    for _, key, value in out:
        if value is monkeypatch.notset:
            mp.delenv(key, False)
        else:
            mp.setenv(key, value)

    yield out
    mp.undo()
```

CODE 7.14   Change environment variables with monkey patch.

monkeypatch provides the *delenv()* and *setenv()* functions to delete and set environment variables.

Similarly, you can even change the system paths visible to Python. The fixture defined in code snippet 7.15 prepends the *test_apps'* path to the system PATH environment variable so it will be picked up by Python first.

```
@pytest.fixture
def test_apps(monkeypatch):
    monkeypatch.syspath_prepend(os.path.join(os.path.dirname(__
file__), "test_apps"))
    original_modules = set(sys.modules.keys())

    yield

    for key in sys.modules.keys() - original_modules:
        sys.modules.pop(key)
```

CODE 7.15   Change *PATH* with monkey patch.

Remember that we have the *setUp()* and *tearDown()* functions from unittest that behave like coroutines. This pytest fixture is just a coroutine. Whatever before the *yield* is like the *setUp* and whatever after that is like the *tearDown()*.

We didn't teardown our *print* function replacement earlier because we only have one test to run. If there are multiple tests in a test session like the flask's, you don't want the *test_apps* to be visible to other unrelated tests.

One last monkey patch example comes from matplotlib library. We discussed the lazy creation of axis ticks earlier. In the test *test_compare_images*,[5] we change the current working directory to a temporary directory and do all kinds of crazy stuff there. I will leave the details to yourself but its central line code snippet 7.16.

```
monkeypatch.chdir(tmp_path)
```

CODE 7.16   Use monkeypatch to change the directory.

Next, let's move on to another important topic that is commonly missed in testing discussion.

PROPERTY-BASED TEST

Let's look at our test more closely. We take several positive integers, pass them to the tested function and compare the results with pre-obtained, expected results.

Regardless of the usage of fixture and monkey patch, what we have done so far are example-based tests. Basically, we pre-pick a few test examples and make sure the function works for these examples.

What if an *evil* developer just wrote a function like code snippet 7.17 to pass those tests?

```
class PrimeFactorizer:
    def __init__(self):
        pass

    def prime_factors(self, n):
        if n == 2:
            return [2]
        elif n == 12:
            return [2, 2, 3]
        elif:
            #skip
```

CODE 7.17   A function that is designed to cheat the test.

Well, we can add more test cases, probably more difficult ones. No engineers won't be able to eyeball the prime factors of 345,234,139,217. I made up this random number while I was writing this book. It is perhaps a good idea to randomize the example input.

However, to implement this *brilliant* idea, we will have to implement a prime factorization method in our test! We can be creative to avoid the trial division method. The ugly truth is that we are reinventing wheels in our test.

Can we test without introducing examples?

The right direction is to test the property of our function. A property of a result is independent of specific examples but intrinsic to the core of the algorithm or application.

For example, based on the way we write the *prime _ factorizer()* method, our result must have the following *properties*.

1. The return is a list of integers, unless the input is 1.

2. Every integer in this list divides the input exactly,

3. The integers are arranged in an increasing order.

4. Every integer is a prime number.

5. The product of the integers is exactly the input.

The idea of property testing is that we randomly create some examples and check against those properties. Fortunately, there is already a library called *hypothesis* that does most of the job for us. Code snippet 7.18 is an example of using the hypothesis library.

```
from hypothesis import given
from hypothesis import strategies as st

class TestPrimeFactorizer:
    @given(st.integers(min_value=1, max_value=10000))
    def test_prime_factors_property(self, n):
        factorizer = PrimeFactorizer()
```

```
        factors = factorizer.prime_factors(n)

        assert n == 1 or len(factors) > 0
        assert all(isinstance(f, int) for f in factors)
        assert all(f > 1 for f in factors)
        assert n == 1 or all(n % factor == 0 for factor in factors)
        assert n == 1 or all([factor] == factorizer.prime_
factors(factor) for factor in factors)
        assert all(factors[i] <= factors[i + 1] for i in
range(len(factors) - 1))
        assert n == 1 or n == reduce(lambda x, y: x * y, factors)
```

CODE 7.18   Use hypothesis to test the *prime _ factors()*.

hypothesis provides two basic objects called *given* and *strategies. given* is essentially a decorator that takes a strategy as input to generate test samples for the decorated function to use.

The *strategies* module provides a wide range of functions to define the input space of the function. In our example above, we use the *integers* strategy and limit the lower bound and upper bound of the inputs.

hypothesis library provides a wide range of possibilities of strategies, and you can combine them to build your own. Code 7.19 is a customized strategy for the demo purpose.

```
from hypothesis import strategies as st

my_tuple_strategy = st.builds(
    tuple,
    st.integers(min_value=0, max_value=100),
    st.text(min_size=1, max_size=10)
)

my_list_strategy = st.lists(my_tuple_strategy, min_size=1)
```

CODE 7.19   A customized *strategy.*

First, we create a strategy that binds an integer and a string to a tuple. We also specify the bounds of the integers and the length of the string. Then, we build another strategy that creates a list of such tuples with a minimal size of 1. Such flexibility makes strategy building very powerful for generating test data so we can focus on the properties without worrying about the *evil* developer's crafting.

Back to the factorization test, disregarding the special case 1, we first test that the returned list must contain at least one factor. The factors must all be integers greater than 1. The factors must all divide the input. The factors must be arranged in an increasing order and their product must match the input.

The interesting test is that we reuse our tested function to check whether each factor is a prime number. If it is a prime number, then we should get a list of one member: itself. This is not enough to say that the factor is *in fact* a prime number, but it does prove that the *prime _ factors()* is self-consistent. If you pass a prime number to it, it will always return the prime number itself in a list.

Writing a property-based testing usually requires deeper insights into the problem you were trying to solve. It can help you find bugs that you might not have thought to test for manually, as well as increase the coverage of your tests. Property-based testing can also help you identify edge cases and boundary conditions that your code may not handle properly.

However, property-based testing is not always fancy. There are low-hanging, property-based tests like a there-and-back test. If you are writing something that converts A to B, then converting it back from B should give A back exactly. This is a very common test that you can find in libraries like *xarray*.[6]

xarray is a Python library that provides a way to work with labeled multi-dimensional arrays and labeled multi-dimensional datasets. It is built on top of numpy. A natural task is to convert an xarray object to a pandas DataFrame. The *test_ pandas_roundtrip. py*[7] file does the job exactly.

For example, the test in snippet 7.20 converts a dataset with 1d variables to a pandas DataFrame and then converts it back. The roundtripped result must be exactly the same as the original one.

```
@given(datasets_1d_vars())
def test_roundtrip_dataset(dataset) -> None:
    df = dataset.to_dataframe()
    assert isinstance(df, pd.DataFrame)
    roundtripped = xr.Dataset(df)
    xr.testing.assert_identical(dataset, roundtripped)
```

CODE 7.20   pandas DataFrame round trip test.

Here, *datasets _ 1d _ vars()* is a customized strategy. It is defined as in snippet 7.21. The creation of an xarray object is like a pandas DataFrame: we specify an index and a dictionary object that determines the *column* name and values.

```
@st.composite
def datasets_1d_vars(draw) -> xr.Dataset:
    idx = draw(pdst.indexes(dtype="u8", min_size=0, max_size=100))

    vars_strategy = st.dictionaries(
        keys=st.text(),
        values=npst.arrays(dtype=numeric_dtypes, shape=len(idx)).
map(
            partial(xr.Variable, ("rows",))
        ),
```

```
        min_size=1,
        max_size=3,
    )
    return xr.Dataset(draw(vars_strategy), coords={"rows": idx})
```

CODE 7.21   Creation of a 1-d xarray dataset.

The *strategies.composite* is another decorator that provides more powerful strategy building. You can use the *draw* function to draw values from other strategies within the composite strategy. In this example, the *pdst* variable is a strategy that stands for *hypothesis.extra.pandas*. It is like an *extension module* from the hypothesis library that allows you to generate data for some common data types.

SUMMARY

In summary, fixture, parameterization, monkey patch, and property-based testing are essential techniques in Python testing. Fixtures provide a way to share code between tests, while parameterization allows for testing of multiple inputs with a single test function. Monkey patching is useful for modifying objects and attributes during testing, while property-based testing uses generated input to ensure that code behaves correctly under a wide range of scenarios. These techniques improve testing efficiency and coverage, allowing for more robust and reliable code.

NOTES

1 https://github.com/psf/requests/blob/main/tests/test_requests.py#L94
2 https://github.com/omnilib/aiosqlite/blob/main/aiosqlite/tests/smoke.py
3 https://github.com/pallets/flask
4 https://github.com/pallets/flask/blob/main/tests/conftest.py
5 https://github.com/matplotlib/matplotlib/blob/main/lib/matplotlib/tests/test_compare_images.py
6 https://docs.xarray.dev/en/stable/
7 https://github.com/pydata/xarray/blob/main/properties/test_pandas_roundtrip.py

Index

Note: **Bold** page numbers refer to tables; *italic* page numbers refer to figures.